GREAT
LINEBACKERS

GREAT
LINEBACKERS

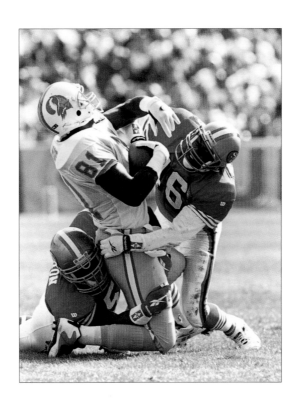

STEPHEN MAJEWSKI

MetroBooks

MetroBooks

An Imprint of Friedman/Fairfax Publishers

© 1997 by Michael Friedman Publishing Group, Inc.

Library of Congress Cataloging-in-Publication Data

Majewski, Stephen.
    Great linebackers / Stephen Majewski
         p.   cm.
    Includes index.
    Summary: Describes the position of linebacker and includes interviews with fifteen of football's greatest linebackers.
    ISBN 1-56799-484-9 (hc)
    1. Linebackers (Football)—United States—Biography.
2. Football—Defense.
[1. Football players.] 1.Title.
GV939.A1M36   1997
796.332'23'0922—dc21
[B]   97-9044

Editors: Ben Boyington and Stephen Slaybaugh
Art Director: Kevin Ullrich
Designer: Diego Vainesman
Photography Editor: Amy Talluto

Color separations by HK Scanner Arts Int'l Ltd.
Printed in Hong Kong by Wing King Tong Co Ltd

10 9 8 7 6 5 4 3 2 1

For bulk purchases and special sales, please contact:
Friedman/Fairfax Publishers
Attention: Sales Department
15 West 26th Street
New York, NY 10010
212/685-6610 FAX 212/685-1307

Visit our website:
http://www.metrobooks.com

DEDICATION

For James David "Buddy" Ryan

ACKNOWLEDGMENTS

Thank you to all the people who helped get this book completed: my wife Libby Majewski, the NFL's public relations department, the Pro Football Hall of Fame, pro football's great linebackers, and Stephen Slaybaugh. I would also like to thank all the excellent sports writers whose books, articles, and essays provided invaluable insights into professional football and the position of linebacker.

CONTENTS

INTRODUCTION

If the National Football League were an army, then its linebackers would be the Green Beret Special Forces. With their size, strength, speed, quickness, and agility, linebackers have the physical attributes to defeat nearly any enemy and overcome almost any obstacle. They also have the intelligence to diagnose enemy movements and formations. What is more important, linebackers possess a killer instinct that is essential for battle. Future Hall of Fame linebacker Lawrence Taylor, for instance, used to talk of his "kill hits": "It's when you hit the quarterback so hard that he's out there quivering on the ground and stuff's coming out his nose."

Former Los Angeles Rams and Washington Redskins head coach George Allen believed that linebackers are the most important players on defense. Looking around the NFL today, it's difficult to disagree with that belief. Junior Seau, Derrick Thomas, Hardy Nickerson, Greg Lloyd, Bryce Paup, and Bryan Cox, to name only a few, are not only some of the best linebackers in the game but also some of the top players in the league.

Linebackers perform vital roles as the connecting links between the defensive linemen and the defensive backs. The defensive linemen have to stop the run and pressure the quarterback so that he has less time to find his receivers. The defensive backs have to cover the receivers so that the defensive linemen can get to the quarterback. If the linebackers don't do a little bit of everything—stop the run, pressure the quarterback, and cover the receivers—the entire defense will fall apart.

These various responsibilities make linebacker one of the most exciting positions in football. Linebackers can showcase their versatility more than other defensive players—they get more opportunities than defensive backs to sack the quarterback and more chances than defensive linemen to intercept the football. Interceptions as well as forcing and

A torn right bicep muscle suffered during the second half of the 1993 season couldn't stop Ken Norton (51) from starting every game for the Dallas Cowboys. That same year, Dallas won its second consecutive Super Bowl championship.

ABOVE: **The most versatile linebackers can cover the pass. Here, Bryan Cox (51) tackles tight end Pete Metzelaars.**

OPPOSITE: **Lawrence Taylor (56) was one of the few defensive players in pro football history who could dictate the outcome of a game.**

recovering fumbles provide linebackers with many chances to score.

In an age in which many players specialize in stopping the run or covering the pass, the best linebackers in the NFL have the versatility to play every down. Linebackers such as the San Francisco 49ers' Ken Norton, the Arizona Cardinals' Eric Hill, and the St. Louis Rams' Roman Phifer are equally adept against the run and the pass and they play every down. "People say Junior Seau's all over the field. Phifer's the same way," said former Rams safety Anthony Newman. "If it's a run, he's in on the run. If it's a pass twenty yards downfield, he's downfield on the tackle."

It's difficult to imagine, but at one time linebackers were only peripheral members of the defense. Before the mid 1950s, the standard defensive formation consisted of five defensive linemen, two linebackers, and four defensive backs. In the two-way system of that era, the linebackers were generally offensive players who provided defensive support to the defensive line. By the late 1950s, specialization had replaced the two-way system and the four-three alignment (four defensive linemen, three linebackers, and four defensive backs) had replaced the five-two formation. Linebackers, especially middle linebackers, began to achieve a status of their own. It was a television documentary, however, that

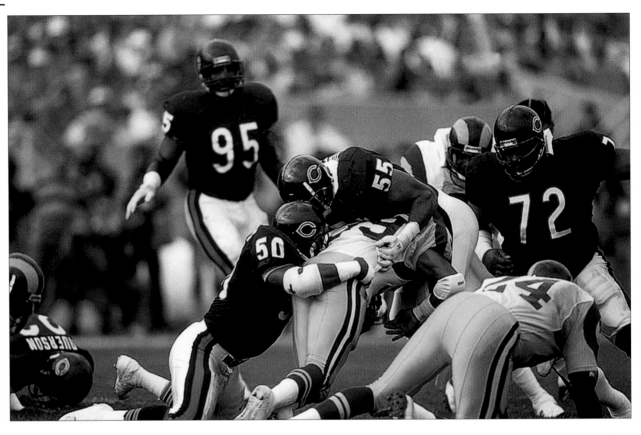

Though he wasn't the biggest or strongest middle linebacker, Mike Singletary (50) was the quintessential leader on the field.

helped to create the image of the linebacker as a tough, aggressive, loyal warrior.

"The Violent World of Sam Huff" aired at 6:30 P.M. on Sunday, October 30, 1960. Hosted by Walter Cronkite, this half-hour CBS documentary gave America its first up-close view of professional football. New York Giants middle linebacker Sam Huff was the focus of the show: a news camera followed the linebacker, who wore a microphone on the front of his shoulder pads, through a few weeks of training camp and a preseason game against the Chicago Bears.

For the first time, viewers got to hear the sounds of professional football: players calling offensive and defensive signals, pads colliding, players groaning, and teammates cheering. Profanity, of course, was cut. "Anytime you play football on the field there is no place for nice guys," Huff told the audience. "I always feel real good when I hit someone. You just hear that leather thud in there and you feel that you've accomplished something. You've made a beautiful tackle."

In the days before instant replays, super-slow motion, and on-field microphones, the effects of the show were astounding. One out of every four television sets in America was tuned to "Violent World." Middle linebacker became a glamorous position, and Huff became professional football's first celebrated defensive player. Since then, with the careers of such players as Dick Butkus, Ray Nitschke, and Mike Singletary, the linebacker has taken on mythical proportions.

The specific tasks of a linebacker depend on whether his team plays a four-three defense or a three-four defense and whether he is a middle linebacker, an inside linebacker, or an outside linebacker. Despite their differences, however, all linebackers share common responsibilities that make them the most versatile players in football. They all must stop the run, cover the pass, and rush the quarterback. Linebackers must also have the intelligence to read offenses.

Many offensive plays are designed to neutralize the linebacker. The play-action pass is designed to make the linebacker commit to the run so that a receiver can get open behind him. The draw play is designed to make the linebacker commit to the pass so that a running back can run in the vacated territory. Many passing plays are designed to force a slower linebacker to cover a faster receiver or a smaller linebacker to cover a bigger tight end.

Each linebacker keys, or focuses, on a particular offensive player for the first indication of where the play is going. Although no two linebackers key in exactly the same manner, there are some general guidelines. The middle linebacker usually keys on the center, the two guards, and the formation of the running backs. The strong-side linebacker (the linebacker opposite the tight end) keys on the tight end. His secondary keys are the guard and running back closest to him. The weak-side linebacker usually keys on the tackle, guard, and running back closest to him.

If a linebacker fails to read the correct key or makes obvious which player he is keying on, the quarterback will use the keyed-on player as a decoy. For example, if it is obvious that the middle linebacker is keying on the fullback and ignoring the center and guards, the quarterback might send the fullback on a fake running play to the left side. With the middle of the field open, the real ballcarrier—the tailback—has the opportunity for a substantial gain.

"When you say a quarterback is out to fool the defense, what you mean is that a quarterback is out to fool the linebackers," said former Green Bay Packers outside linebacker Dave Robinson. "The quarterback knows what the front four will do: rush. He doesn't have time to fool the deep backs. He's out to make three linebackers think pass, or he's out to make you think run."

In the four-three defense, everything starts with the middle linebacker calling the defensive signals. Therefore the middle linebacker must not only have the agility to avoid 300-pound (136kg) blockers, the strength to move in to the line of scrimmage to stop running plays, the speed to cover receivers, and the desire to tackle ballcarriers, but also the intelligence to diagnose offensive formations.

Kevin Greene (91) gets one of his NFL-leading 14 sacks in 1994. As a Carolina Panther in 1996, Greene led the league in sacks again with 14.5.

Once he reads the offense and sets the defense, the middle linebacker has more freedom than players at other positions to roam the field in search of prey. He reads his keys at the snap and then simply goes after the ball. A good middle linebacker is involved in almost two out of every three plays. The San Diego Chargers' Junior Seau explained the middle linebacker's mission when he said flatly, "If there's a football on the field, I'm going after it."

The outside linebacker's responsibilities depend on whether he plays in a four-three or three-four defense and whether he lines up on the strong side or the weak side. In the four-three, an outside linebacker needs speed to cover receivers and strength to ward off 290-pound (132kg) guards on sweeps. On running plays, the outside linebacker's job is to force the run back to the inside. On passing plays, the weak-side linebacker usually covers running backs because he is lighter and faster than the strong-side linebacker. The Philadelphia

13

Eagles' William Thomas is one of the best pass-covering linebackers in the NFL. His seven interceptions in 1995 topped all linebackers that year.

The Arizona Cardinals' Seth Joyner is another excellent outside linebacker. In this age of specialization, Joyner is a complete linebacker. He can blitz, stop the run, and cover the pass. He plays the pass so well that the Cardinals moved him to strong safety for a few games in 1995 to help their injury-ravaged secondary. "He's a coach's dream because he can do everything," said former Raiders tight end and current television analyst Todd Christensen. "Joyner can blitz, play over the tight end, and support the run."

The outside linebacker actually has more to worry about than the middle linebacker. "On the outside," said former Oakland Raiders head coach and current Fox television analyst John Madden, "a linebacker has to worry about different blocking combinations. If the tight end blocks down on the defensive end, he may have to fill that gap. He may have to take on the pulling guard or a blocking back. Or in a passing situation, he may have to slow up the tight end." Although outside linebackers have many responsibilities, their position on the field gives them the advantage of seeing everything unfold. They can see the play develop and position themselves to deliver a big hit.

In the 1970s and 1980s, many teams switched from the four-three defense to a three-four scheme. The Miami Dolphins were one of the first teams to make the change. Miami defensive coordinator Bill Arnsparger inserted Bob Matheson as a fourth linebacker in place of a defensive lineman. This defense was called the 53 because Matheson's jersey number was 53. Matheson had the strength to stop the run and the speed to cover receivers. Miami went a perfect 17–0 in the 1972 season using the three-four defense.

Junior Seau (55) reads his keys before flying to the ballcarrier.

Inside linebackers in a three-four defense are bulkier than their outside counterparts. Three-four inside linebackers have responsibilities similar to those of four-three middle linebackers. On running plays, they must help the nose tackle clog the middle. On passing plays, they must cover running backs and tight ends, but they usually don't drop as deep as four-three linebackers. Because of the prominence

of outside linebackers in the three-four defense, inside linebackers get little recognition. Nonetheless, three-four inside linebackers are important because they make many tackles. Two of the best in recent history include the New York Giants' Harry Carson and the Denver Broncos' Karl Mecklenburg. The Carolina Panthers' Sam Mills is one of the top inside linebackers in the game today.

Most outside linebackers are pass rushers in the three-four defense. Big, strong, mobile, and fast, they are often the best athletes on a football team. The three-four outside linebacker's primary job is to pressure the quarterback. Most of these players line up on the weak side, where they battle running backs, tackles, and even tight ends to get to the quarterback. The prototype pass-rushing linebacker was Lawrence Taylor, who was the NFL's second all-time sack leader when he retired.

Ironically, the three-four defense is similar to the five-two defense of yesteryear. "Most outside linebackers that go to the Pro Bowl are just blitzers," said Arizona Cardinals head coach Buddy Ryan. "They're like stand-up defensive ends." The cyclical world of professional football has seen a return by most teams to the four-three defense in the 1990s.

Although they are taught to read keys, the best linebackers, regardless of their specific position, read the entire offense and react to a play instantly. Coaches like to refer to this ability as "football instinct." In reality, this is not instinct but the result of game experience and countless hours of film study. San Diego Chargers general manager Bobby Beathard believes that the ability to react instantly to a play is the most important quality for a linebacker. "If that's not there, then everything else will fall apart," he said. "It's more important than any other position. A defensive back has a cushion of a few yards. For a defensive lineman, it's get off the ball and go. But a linebacker has no margin for misreading. If his instant diagnostic ability isn't there, then he's dead."

A linebacker's intelligence and wisdom play a strong role in his instant reaction to the ball. Before the ball is snapped he considers the game situation, the down and distance, and the field position. Then he looks over the offensive formation for subtle hints. Perhaps a guard inches one foot back in preparation for a sweep or the tight end lines up slightly farther from the tackle in preparation for a passing play. Maybe the quarterback keeps his feet parallel for a running play and one foot farther back for a passing play. Some linebackers even try to hear the quarterback calling the play in the huddle or read his lips. After the play begins, however, a linebacker cannot take the time to think about what he has to do to stop the ballcarrier. Hall of Fame middle linebacker Dick Butkus was a student of football who probably studied game plans and films more than any other player of his time. Once the ball was snapped, however, his thinking ceased. "I know one thing," Butkus said. "You can't think much out there. You've got to react quickly. If you take time to think, you're a dead duck."

Vince Lombardi used to give his players a written test on the Packers' upcoming opponent. Ray Nitschke, one of the greatest middle linebackers in NFL history, consistently bombed these tests but played brilliantly. After Nitschke was married, he aced the tests but his play declined slightly. Lombardi thought he knew why. "Nitschke, I wish you'd break up this marriage of yours," the Packers' head coach joked. "When you were single and sleeping on park benches and getting drunk, you never had the answers right but you played like hell. Now that wife of yours is making you study. So you get the answers right, and you're playing like an old woman."

ABOVE: **Andre Tippett (56) was the most dominating defensive player in the AFC in 1985. That year, the New England Patriots made their first Super Bowl appearance.**

OPPOSITE: **Derrick Thomas (58) is the NFL's premier pass-rushing linebacker. Here, Thomas sacks Warren Moon in a 1994 playoff game.**

CHAPTER ONE
THE LINEBACKER MENTALITY

Even though linebackers play in the middle and on the outside, on the strong side and the weak side, and in the four-three and the three-four, they are united by a unique psyche that separates them from other football players. "From the first day of practice, I could always tell who my linebackers were," said former New York Jets assistant coach Joe Haering. "I'd take my best defensive players and smack them in the head. The ones that smacked me back were linebackers."

Haering's tale may be apocryphal, but it illustrates the linebacker mentality perfectly. Hit them and they'll hit you. Hurt them and they'll hurt you. Try to kill them and they'll try to kill you. Linebackers are born with a street-fighter's attitude that is appeased only by hitting and tackling. The drive to inflict pain on ballcarriers is what motivates linebackers. "You want to punish the running backs," said Pittsburgh Steelers outside linebacker Greg Lloyd. "You like to kick them and, when they get down, kick them again until they wave the white flag."

Intensity and toughness are necessities for a linebacker, who gets hit on every play and whose job is only half over when he's beaten an offensive lineman or a blocking back. After those chores, a linebacker not only has to make the tackle but also has to intimidate the ballcarrier so that he doesn't want to run the ball anymore. Only an intense, tough, and slightly crazy person can handle the pressure of being constantly bludgeoned on every Sunday afternoon for six months of the year.

Lloyd and Kevin Greene made up the National Football League's most intense linebacking tandem when they played together with the Steelers. "Kevin Greene is from somewhere else. He's not from here," said cornerback LeRoy Irvin, Greene's former teammate with the Los Angeles Rams. "That guy is about chain of command, hitting the beaches, dropping the napalm bombs, guerrilla warfare. You have to understand his lingo. He's a different breed of cat, no doubt." Greene agreed: "I'm intense, but I guess that's just part of the linebacker mentality."

The best linebackers are good tacklers and hard hitters. San Francisco 49ers outside linebacker Lee Woodall is one of the NFL's surest tacklers, but he also packs a punch. "When he hits you, he hits you with a load, and he gets you down," said 49ers defensive coordinator John Marshall. "He would like to put you down where you're not going to get up. He's got a great linebacker's mentality."

"That's true," agreed Woodall. "I love to hit and I love to punish people. If I can hurt a guy on a tackle, I can punish him and I can make him cringe, or I can make him think about running toward me, I love it."

The exaltation of a bone-crushing tackle was a football epiphany for former Chicago Bears middle linebacker Mike Singletary. "The resultant feeling," Singletary said, "has always been almost indescribable to me, akin to being struck, I suppose, by a bolt of lightning—a blast that, for one brief second, shines through your mind and body like a flash of brilliant white heat."

Mention tough linebackers and names such as Bryan Cox and Lawrence Taylor come to mind. Some say, however, that the toughest football player in NFL

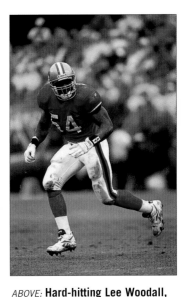

ABOVE: **Hard-hitting Lee Woodall, a sixth-round pick, was the steal of the 1994 NFL draft. Woodall won a starting position and helped the San Francisco 49ers win Super Bowl XXIX.**

OPPOSITE: **A musician off the field, Jimmie Williams made sweet music with a bone-crushing tackle on gameday.**

Greg Lloyd (95) prefers the big hit, but he'll do whatever it takes to bring down the ballcarrier.

history was San Francisco 49ers linebacker Hardy "the Hatchet" Brown. The six-foot (183cm), 195-pound (88kg) Brown enjoyed driving his right shoulder up into a ballcarrier's chin. Hall of Fame quarterback Y.A. Tittle said that in 1951 Brown "knocked out the entire Washington Redskins starting backfield, everyone except Harry Gilmer, the quarterback. He retired [Los Angeles Rams halfback] Glenn Davis—hit him so hard in the head he tore ligaments in Davis's knee. Did the same thing to [Detroit Lions end] Bill Swiacki the next year. Hardy Brown was the hardest hitter that ever played."

Although linebackers thrive on punishing ballcarriers, they also experience a strange delight when they feel pain. In a 1992 game against the Cleveland Browns, Lloyd beat two blockers before meeting running back Kevin Mack at the line of scrimmage. The blow staggered Lloyd, who is a second-degree black belt in tae kwon do. "I was dizzy, my head was hurting, and my eyes were watering," said Lloyd. "It felt good." It's no wonder that Lawrence Taylor once said, "Show me good linebackers and I'll show you some strange mental profiles."

Linebackers combine their uncivilized brutality with a fierce loyalty and a skewed sense of justice. In their violent world, injustices to teammates are righted with wrathful vengeance. When linebacker Bryan Cox was a rookie with the Miami Dolphins, he witnessed a Bengals linebacker plowing over Dolphins kicker Pete Stoyanovich on a kickoff. Cox immediately charged Cincinnati's sideline and challenged everybody on the bench to a fight.

"I noticed that the linebacker who hit Pete was laughing," recalled Cox. "So I suggested if he wanted to hit somebody bigger, he ought to go ahead and hit me. Well, he stopped laughing." As for the wisdom of taking on the entire Bengals team, "They all could've gotten me," Cox added, "but I would've gotten somebody. And he would have remembered me."

Even though linebackers go after ballcarriers like heat-seeking missiles, they must also play intelligently and under control. Playing middle linebacker, for instance, requires intelligence to position everybody correctly, call the right coverage, and still be able to make plays. If linebackers are overaggressive, they become susceptible to fakes and trick plays.

In the mid 1980s, the Chicago Bears had one of the most fearsome defenses in NFL history. Outside linebacker Wilber Marshall could knock out a quarterback as easily as he could blanket a receiver downfield. The Bears, however, led by Singletary, took a cerebral approach to the game. "What we're proving," Singletary said at the time, "is that it's possible to think and play defense at the same time."

Intense, tough, brutal, loyal, and intelligent, linebackers are at once complicated and simple. Within a split second of trying to read an offense cogently, linebackers attack ballcarriers with the savagery of a hungry tiger. That most linebackers are mild-mannered citizens off the field makes understanding them no easier. Former Cincinnati Bengals linebacker Reggie Williams epitomized this Dr. Jekyll and Mr. Hyde nature. On Sundays, Williams created chaos on the gridiron. For the remainder of the week, he sought order and justice as a city councilman.

When Mike Curtis patrolled the middle of field for the Baltimore Colts, he was known as "Animal" or "Mad Dog." During a game, Curtis played with the viciousness of these nicknames. On one occasion, he even decked a Baltimore fan who ran onto the playing field and picked up the football. When not playing middle linebacker, however, Curtis preferred the idyllic solitude of his farm in Virginia. "From the back windows you can gaze peacefully at the Blue Ridge Mountains of Virginia," he said. "The view of the Blue Ridge is more beautiful than ever in autumn, with the mountains exploding with color as the leaves change in the early November days."

Former Detroit Lions outside linebacker Jimmie Williams played the tenor saxophone to relax himself. "It gives me," he said, "an inner peace and serenity." On

Kevin Greene admits that he will not know what to do with himself when his days of chasing quarterbacks are over.

the field, however, Williams was anything but tranquil. "If it's between getting an interception and putting a hit on the receiver," he said, "I'll always hit the receiver. I like to hit the man and hear that little moan."

The Buffalo Bills' Bryce Paup, the 1995 NFL Defensive Player of the Year, has experienced a linebacker's worst nightmare. Despite his intimidating six-foot-five-inch (196cm), 245-pound (111kg) frame, Paup's reputation was that of a family man who gave it his all as soon as he stepped on the football field. The last thing a linebacker wants is to be considered sensitive or caring. They prefer the image of a gangster who would just as soon kill you as look at you. To solve his dilemma, Paup got a flattop haircut. "I wanted to look meaner," he said. "Everybody thought I was a nice guy who played hard, and I wanted to change that image."

Though they want to be considered mean and nasty, even the toughest linebackers are capable of having their feelings hurt. Former Philadelphia Eagles defensive halfback and broadcaster Tom Brookshier once began a postgame interview with the Green Bay Packers' Ray Nitschke, who was never considered a paragon of civility on the field, by introducing him as the "madman of Green Bay." Offended, Nitschke replied, "I am not an animal!"

Perhaps no two players exemplify the dual nature of linebackers more than the San Diego Chargers' Junior Seau and the Kansas City Chiefs' Derrick Thomas. Seau

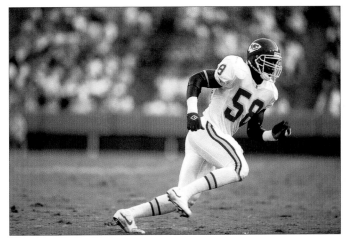

ABOVE: **After an unspectacular but solid season in 1995, Derrick Thomas (58) came back to make 13 sacks in 1996.**

OPPOSITE: **Before becoming a dominating pass rusher for the Buffalo Bills, mild-mannered Bryce Paup (95) played all four linebacker positions for the Green Bay Packers. Here, Paup stuffs the Rams' Cleveland Gary for a safety.**

and Thomas are two of the NFL's most dominating linebackers. Both have been named NFL Man of the Year for their on-the-field performance and off-the-field charitable works. These two men want to make a difference not only on the field but also in their community. "Too many athletes are living in a tiny window," Seau said. "They have no vision for themselves—what they can be outside of football and what they can mean to a community. My hopes and dreams are unlimited."

Thomas shares Seau's attitude. "Sure, I'd like to be remembered for what I did on the field and maybe one day have an opportunity to make it into Canton," said Thomas. "But I'd also like to be remembered for the things I did off the field when I was in a position to make a difference."

These philanthropic comments sound paradoxical coming from men who froth at the mouth when they have a chance to blindside a quarterback. That, however, is the linebacker mentality.

CHAPTER TWO
MIDDLE LINEBACKER:
Quaterback of the Defense

On offense, everything starts with the quarterback. He gets the play from the coaches on the sideline, tells his teammates the play in the huddle, diagnoses the opposition, calls the signals at the line of scrimmage—perhaps changing the original play if he sees something in the opposition's formation that warrants a different plan of attack—and takes the snap from the center.

On most National Football League teams, the middle linebacker goes through the exact same steps as the quarterback, with the exception, of course, of taking the snap from the center. In effect, the middle linebacker is the quarterback of the defense. Like the quarterback, the middle linebacker must be a leader. He must convince his teammates that they are better than they really are. He must always be aware of his team's personnel. He must understand each player's defensive assignment so that he can make the proper audible, depending on the offensive formation.

Sophisticated NFL offenses force the middle linebacker to make adjustments right up to the snap of the ball. When a running back moves into a slot or a wide receiver goes into motion, it forces the defense to change. NFL defenses, however, are also equally sophisticated. The middle linebacker can choose from a large inventory of formations and options to stymie the offense's maneuvers.

As the game progresses, the middle linebacker must recognize patterns in the offense's game plan. Perhaps he realizes that the running game is directed at a slightly injured defensive player on the left side of the field. To compensate for that weakness, the middle linebacker can revise the defensive strategy to counteract the offense and help the exploited player.

To lead the defense successfully, the middle linebacker must have a good idea beforehand of what the opposition is going to do. That means hours of studying films and reading game plans and scouting reports. Future Hall of Fame middle linebacker Mike Singletary made film study his trademark. On hearing that former Philadelphia Eagles head coach Dick Vermeil once ran a single play back fifty-two times, Singletary replied, "I don't want to brag, but [my wife] will vouch for the fact that I've exceeded that limit on many, many occasions."

OPPOSITE: **Mike Singletary (50) studied countless hours of film so he could immediately recognize the offensive formation and call a counterplay.**

BELOW: **Nick Buoniconti (85) directed the Miami Dolphins' "No-Name Defense" to consecutive victories in Super Bowls VII and VIII.**

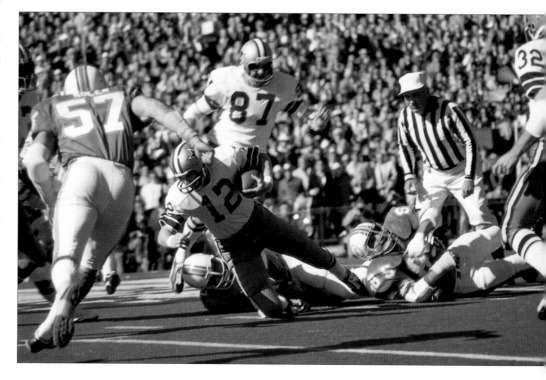

Films show not only the opposition's specific plays, but also how players react in various situations. For instance, if the Buffalo Bills are to meet the Indianapolis Colts, Bills inside linebacker Chris Spielman—a four-time Pro Bowl selection at middle linebacker—will study film of the Colts' previous game. He will analyze the entire Indianapolis offense to see how the Colts prefer to attack defenses. Spielman will also pay close attention to the Colts' center to see if there are any weaknesses that he can exploit.

The middle linebacker's work is not done after he has called the defense—not by a long shot. When the ball is snapped, the middle linebacker must instantly make the correct read of pass or run, fight off 300-pound (136kg) offensive linemen trying to pancake-block him, and then pursue the ball. If he misreads the play or pauses for even a split second, he's finished. Former Philadelphia Eagles and Arizona Cardinals head coach Buddy Ryan believes that at certain times, such as during running plays, the middle linebacker has a more difficult job than the quarterback. "After the quarterback turns around and hands the ball off, his job is basically over," says Ryan. "But a middle linebacker has to read run or pass. He's going all the time."

On running plays, the middle linebacker must either make the tackle or force the ball-carrier toward a teammate who can tackle that player. On passing plays, he is responsible for covering the tight end or the running backs. The middle linebacker must always be ready for the draw play or the screen pass. If the draw is run late, the middle linebacker must run back

Like quarterbacks, middle linebackers can be judged by the success of their teams. Ken Norton has been the middle linebacker of three Super Bowl champions.

from his deep position, get rid of any blockers, and make the tackle or force the play to someone else. On a screen, the middle linebacker has to take on the screen of blockers and, again, make the tackle or force the ball-carrier toward a teammate. Both of these plays are challenges to the best middle linebackers.

Leadership becomes vital in the middle linebacker's important role of quarterback of the defense. "A middle linebacker has to be a leader," said former Miami Dolphins middle linebacker Nick Buoniconti. "His teammates look to him for leadership, and effective play-calling is one means of establishing that leadership."

Winning is another yardstick for measuring leadership, and outstanding middle linebackers have been a part of many of the most powerful teams in NFL history. Sam Huff, Joe Schmidt, Ray Nitschke, Jack Lambert, Ken Norton, and Mike Singletary were the heart and soul of championship defenses. By winning the Super Bowl with the Cowboys in 1992 and 1993 and with the 49ers in 1994, Norton became the first player in NFL history to play for the winning Super Bowl team in three consecutive seasons.

Middle linebackers also can be inspirational leaders in the locker room. Former Miami Dolphins head coach Don Shula received much criticism for his coaching in 1995, a year in which many experts predicted that Miami would win the American Football Conference championship. When Miami's record fell to 7–6, Dolphins middle linebacker Bryan Cox refused to blame the coaches. Instead, he wanted the players to stand up and take responsibility for their performance. "Look," Cox said, "I don't give a damn if Jesus Christ were coaching this team, because we're not playing well. You could have Vince Lombardi, John Madden, or any of those coaches, but you won't win if your players don't perform on game day."

When you consider that there was no such thing as a middle linebacker until the mid 1950s, it's something of an irony that today he is the most important player on defense. But it's true—a defense without a middle linebacker is like an offense without a quaterback.

The Chicago Bears' Bill George is generally credited as the first middle linebacker in NFL history. In the early 1950s, George was a middle guard in the old five-two defense. On passing downs, the middle guard bumped the center before dropping back into pass coverage. During one game in 1954, however, George was regularly getting beaten on passing plays. Instead of first bumping the center, George immediately stood up and took a step off the line of scrimmage. Later in the game, he intercepted a pass, and the position of middle linebacker was born.

The CBS documentary "The Violent World of Sam Huff" helped to make middle linebacker a glamorous position in the eyes of football fans. The position of middle linebacker, however, might never have achieved its mystique if it were not for the defensive innovations of former New York Giants defensive coordinator and Dallas Cowboys head coach Tom Landry.

It was Landry who first envisioned the middle linebacker as the centerpiece of the defense. The middle linebacker, Landry reasoned, ought to receive the same protection from his defensive linemen as the quarterback does from his offensive linemen. Landry wanted his defensive line to shield the middle linebacker from blockers and funnel ballcarriers into the middle of the field. While this defensive strategy prevented long sideline runs, it also allowed the middle linebacker to make most of the tackles.

In the 1950s and 1960s, almost every year that the Giants competed with the Cleveland Browns for the

Eastern Conference title, Sam Huff was the focal point of the Giants defense, and his duels with Browns fullback Jim Brown became legendary. In fact, because of the media hype about Brown the fullback versus Huff the middle linebacker, notoriety was achieved by various other middle linebackers, such as the Detroit Lions' Joe Schmidt, the Green Bay Packers' Ray Nitschke, and the Chicago Bears' Dick Butkus.

Although Schmidt didn't have the savage reputation of Nitschke and Butkus, most football experts agree that Schmidt was the best middle linebacker during the mid 1950s and the early 1960s. His contribution to the position of middle linebacker cannot be overexaggerated. Schmidt was an instinctive middle linebacker who also appreciated the analytical side of football. He scrupulously studied the opposition's offensive formations so that he would be ready to change the defense as necessary. With Schmidt leading Detroit's defense, the Lions won two NFL championships in the 1950s.

Football has always been in Chris Spielman's blood. "I always wanted to be a football player," he once said. "When I was little, G.I. Joes weren't army men. They were football players. Everything was football."

Players such as Huff, Schmidt, Nitschke, and Butkus set the standard for the great middle linebackers of the 1970s—Mike Curtis, Jack Lambert, Willie Lanier, Tommy Nobis, and others. The rise of the three-four defense in the late 1970s and the 1980s saw a decline in the prominence of the middle linebacker. Some experts consider Singletary the last true middle linebacker. The return of the four-three in the 1990s, however, has created a renaissance at the middle linebacker position.

The best middle linebacker in the NFL today is the San Diego Chargers' Junior Seau. If Bill George represents Stone Age Man in the evolutionary scale of football, then Seau is Modern Man. Seau carries on the tradition of the middle linebacker who can stop the run and cover the pass, but his vastly superior speed makes him a lethal weapon. "He can do anything," says Chargers head coach Bobby Ross. "If he didn't get so tired, I'd seriously consider using him as a return guy. To me, he's as complete a player as I've ever been around."

The 49ers' Ken Norton is another excellent middle linebacker. He was the hub of three consecutive victorious Super Bowl defenses—1992, 1993, and 1994—but 1995 was possibly Norton's best season. "I felt Ken had as good a year as any linebacker I ever have worked with," said 49ers defensive coordinator Pete Carroll.

Other outstanding middle linebackers include Bryan Cox, Hardy Nickerson, Jessie Tuggle, and Eric Hill. Interestingly, Seau, Norton, and Cox all entered the NFL as outside linebackers but were converted to middle linebacker. They brought with them the element of athleticism from the outside linebacker position that distinguishes today's middle linebackers from those of the past.

Like many of today's middle linebackers, Bryan Cox (51) began his career as a Pro Bowl outside linebacker.

CHAPTER THREE
THE PASS RUSHERS

Their images are indelibly stamped in the memories of football fans—Lawrence Taylor, Derrick Thomas, or Bryce Paup blasting through a wall of blockers and splattering the quarterback. Unlike when Bobby Bell, Ted Hendricks, and Jack Ham played outside linebacker, today's outside linebackers are primarily pass rushers. In the 1980s and 1990s, outside linebackers have often led either the National Football League or their conference in sacks. Players such as Thomas, Paup, and Ken Harvey have not been elected to the Pro Bowl for their all-around play but for their ability to rush the quarterback. As the sacks have piled up, pass-rushing linebacker has become one of football's most glamorous positions. Two related events converged to create the position of pass rushing linebacker: the rise of the three-four defense and Lawrence Taylor's entry into the NFL.

The three-four defense, which is built around the linebackers, came into prominence in the 1970s and 1980s as defensive coordinators scurried to counter high-powered, wide-open offenses encouraged by rule changes. The three-four defense brought more responsibilities to outside linebackers than did the defense strategies of the 1950s and 1960s. Outside linebackers now had to stop the run like defensive tackles, cover receivers like defensive backs, and rush the quarterback like defensive ends. These responsibilities required unprecedented athletic ability. As a result, the outside linebackers of today are often the best athletes on an NFL team.

The greatest of all pass-rushing linebackers was the New York Giants' Lawrence Taylor. Few players in the history of the NFL have had as big an influence on the game as Taylor. His size, speed, and strength enabled him to perform never-before-seen feats on the football field. Playing on the weak side of the Giants'

Lawrence Taylor (56) was the most dominating pass-rushing linebacker in football history.

three-four defense, on any given play Taylor had the ability to sack the quarterback, plug the hole for no gain, and run step for step with a receiver. Taylor's career changed not only the way linebackers play defense but also how offenses look at linebackers.

Former New York Giants head coach Bill Parcells recalled the impact Taylor had on the NFL even before the end of his rookie season: "What he really did was change the way other teams looked at the Giants defense. By the end of the 1981 season, coaches were drawing up game plans around Lawrence. Their top priority was dealing with this No. 56 who just seemed to be everywhere, whether they were trying to run the ball or trying to pass the ball."

The six-foot-three-inch (191cm), 240-pound (109kg) Taylor played the game like a tornado, wreak-

ing havoc from sideline to sideline. In 1986, he sacked the quarterback 20.5 times, the fourth-highest single-season total. Taylor retired with 132.5 sacks, second on the NFL's all-time list at the time. His play helped the Giants to victory in Super Bowls XXI and XXV. Because of Taylor, every team felt the need to get a big, strong, quick, fast, and athletic outside linebacker. "If you don't have one," New York Giants general manager George Young said, "you'd damn well better get yourself one."

The New England Patriots' Andre Tippett gave the AFC its version of Lawrence Taylor. Tippett, unlike most pass rushers, lined up on the strong side and on passing downs played as a down lineman. Tippett led the AFC in sacks in 1985 with 16.5 and in 1987 with 12.5. In 1984, he recorded 18.5 sacks, second only to New York Jet Mark Gastineau's league-leading 22. The following year the six-foot-three-inch (191cm), 240-pound (109kg) Tippett led the Patriots to their first Super Bowl appearance. For his career, Tippett sacked the quarterback 100 times.

In the late 1980s and early 1990s, the New Orleans Saints had the NFL's best linebacker corps in Pat Swilling, Rickey Jackson, Sam Mills, and Vaughan Johnson. Swilling, whose 17 sacks in 1991 led the NFL, and Jackson had tremendous speed in their primes and were allowed to freelance. They had the ability to charge from the outside and, if necessary, reverse direction to catch a running back from behind. Swilling, now a member of the Oakland Raiders, primarily plays defensive end because of his pass-rushing skills. Similarly, Charles Haley, now a defensive end with the Dallas Cowboys, was a dominating outside linebacker for the 49ers. His 16 sacks in 1990 led the National Football Conference.

The league's best pass-rushing linebacker since Lawrence Taylor has been Derrick Thomas, who joined the Kansas City Chiefs in 1989. Like Taylor, Thomas' speed and strength make him difficult to block. His ten sacks as a rookie earned him the NFL Defensive Rookie of the Year award. The best year for Thomas, however, was 1990. In that season, he set the single-game record for sacks with 7. His total for the season (20) led the league and was the fifth-highest single-season total in NFL history.

In 1993, the Chiefs' coaching staff moved Thomas to "rushbacker," a defensive end-linebacker hybrid position. The experiment, however, failed. "I'm not a defensive end," said the six-foot-three-inch (191cm), 245-pound (111kg) Thomas. "The great defensive ends are big people, like Neil Smith, Bruce Smith, Chris

It usually takes a double team to keep Kevin Greene (91) from getting to the quarterback.

Doleman. I couldn't compete with people in that category." Wisely, the Chiefs returned Thomas to his natural outside linebacker position.

The Pittsburgh Steelers enjoyed the luxury of having two of the NFL's best pass-rushing linebackers in Greg Lloyd and Kevin Greene. Lloyd is an excellent outside linebacker who has not allowed his pass-rushing assignments to hurt his overall game. He has the strength to stop the run and the speed to cover receivers on passing downs. Greene has been used primarily as a pass rusher. In 1995, the deadly combination of Lloyd (6.5 sacks, 3 interceptions, and 6 forced fumbles) and Greene (9.5 sacks) helped the Steelers earn their fifth Super Bowl appearance.

Lloyd carries on the tradition of the athletic outside linebacker. He stands six feet three inches (191cm) tall, weighs 225 pounds (102kg), and runs the 40 in 4.52 seconds. His body is so well defined that it looks like a masterpiece chiseled in stone. Despite his relatively light weight, however, Lloyd is one of the most feared linebackers in the NFL, as his nickname, "Just Plain Nasty," implies. Lloyd, the 1994 AFC Defensive Player of the Year, is an emotional and intimidating player who doesn't simply want to sack the quarterback, but to "take his ass out of the game."

Greene began his professional career in 1985 with the Los Angeles Rams. He recorded 72.5 sacks in his eight years with the Rams. The Rams, however, leaned toward the four-three in 1991 and Greene's productivity dropped. The six-foot-three-inch (191cm), 250-pound (113kg) Greene signed with the three-four–oriented Steelers as a free agent in 1993. His 14 sacks in 1994 led the NFL, and he was voted the AFC's best linebacker by the NFL Players Association. In 1996, Greene signed a free-agent contract with the Carolina Panthers and again led the league in sacks. By the end of the season, Greene has upped his career sack total to 123.

Greene feels that the thrill of chasing the quarterback will always be in his blood—even after his playing days are over. "I'm going to be lost without the game," he said. "I'm not sure what I'm going to do. I guess I'll end up in a park somewhere late at night and clip somebody while they're drinking water out of a fountain. I'll just come up out of the woods with face paint on or something. Or maybe I'll go low-crawling through the bushes, with a helmet on."

The Buffalo Bills' Bryce Paup is another outside linebacker who has led the league in sacks. Paup has played all four linebacker positions, as well as defensive end, in his career. A sixth-round draft choice of Green Bay in 1990, he racked up 32.5 sacks in four full seasons with the Packers before leaving Green Bay for Buffalo as free agent in 1995.

With Bruce Smith at right defensive end and Cornelius Bennett at right outside linebacker, Paup gave the Bills a much-needed pass rusher from the left side. "All of a sudden our defense was three notches better," said Bills special teams leader Steve Tasker. "Our defensive backfield was playing like it had never played before. We were making interceptions, knocking down passes, getting sacks all over the place."

Paup's 17.5 sacks in 1995 led the league, and he was named the NFL Defensive Player of the Year. "It's nice to get out of the shadows," Paup said on finally getting recognition as a big-time player. "People have always said that I'm doing it because of this or that. It's nice to break out of that. I said all along I'll let other people blow my horn. I'm not going to do it." The addition of Paup helped the Bills improve from 7–9 in 1994 to 10–6 and a playoff berth in 1995.

Ken Harvey has proved that outside linebackers in a four-three defense can also be great blitzers. Harvey has averaged more than 8.5 sacks in nine NFL seasons. The six-foot-two-inch (188cm), 245-pound (111kg) Harvey

began his career with the Phoenix Cardinals in 1988. In 1990, the Cardinals switched to a three-four defense to take advantage of his outstanding athletic ability. Harvey responded with 10 sacks. In 1994, Harvey signed a free-agent contract with Washington. The Redskins play a four-three, but again Harvey didn't miss a beat. His 13.5 sacks that year was tops in the NFC. In 1996, Harvey had another fine year, with 19 sacks.

The return of the four-three defense in the 1990s has not diminished the role of the pass-rushing linebacker. On the contrary, it has produced some of the most versatile linebackers that the league has ever seen. Some of the top middle linebackers in the game—Junior Seau, Ken Norton, and Bryan Cox—are converted outside linebackers. These linebackers are not only excellent run stoppers and pass defenders but also strong blitzers.

Ken Harvey (57) is one of the NFL's best linebackers. He has played well in both the three-four and four-three defenses.

CHAPTER FOUR

MEMORABLE MOMENTS

Offensive players and plays receive much of the glory in National Football League lore. The Immaculate Reception, the Holy Roller, and numerous Hail Marys are part of professional football's canon. Championships, however, are won with defense, and defensive players have been involved in their fair share of memorable moments. Linebackers have been at the center of many of these plays, exemplifying their physical versatility—stopping the run, covering the pass, and rushing the quarterback—and their intangible quality as a ferocious, intimidating warrior.

Not surprisingly, a Hall of Fame linebacker made the most famous tackle in NFL history. It occurred on November 20, 1960, in a contest between the Philadelphia Eagles and the New York Giants at Yankee Stadium. The game was the first of a home-and-home series that figured to decide the Eastern Conference championship. Near the end of this game, with less than two minutes remaining, Philadelphia held a 17–10 lead, but the Giants were on the Eagles' 35-yard line.

On third and ten, Giants halfback Frank Gifford came out of the backfield, ran down the left side of the field, and cut right as he caught George Shaw's pass. He was running for the sideline to stop the clock, unaware that Eagles left outside linebacker Chuck Bednarik was rumbling toward him from his blind side. The six-foot-three-inch (191cm), 235-pound (107kg) Bednarik hit Gifford

Chuck Bednarik celebrates after flattening Frank Gifford with one of the most famous tackles in football lore.

high and hard. Gifford's feet came out from under him, and he landed hard on his head. He also fumbled the football, which Eagles middle linebacker Chuck Weber recovered to seal the victory. Bednarik pumped his fist to celebrate his team's assured win, but Gifford lay motionless and had to be carried off the field on a stretcher. He regained consciousness in the locker room but had suffered a fractured skull and intracranial bleeding.

The hit, Bednarik later recalled, was "like a Volkswagen going down a one-way street and a Mack truck coming the opposite way." It forced Gifford to hang up his shoulder pads for the remainder of the 1960 season and all of 1961. The Eagles defeated the Giants again the following week, 31–23, and went on to win the Eastern Conference title. Bednarik, however, wasn't quite through with his heroics.

The Philadelphia Eagles held a 17–13 lead over the Green Bay Packers in the 1960 NFL Championship game, but Vince Lombardi's troops had the ball on their 35-yard line with 1:30 remaining in the contest. Packers quarterback Bart Starr was having a mediocre day, but he suddenly got hot. Five completions in six attempts put the Packers on the Eagles' 22-yard line with time for just one more play. Starr flipped a screen pass to Jim Taylor, and the powerful fullback set his eyes on the end zone. Taylor broke

two tackles, but Bednarik, despite the exhaustion from playing almost the entire game on offense and defense, was steamrolling to meet him. The two warriors collided at the 9-yard line, where Concrete Charlie wrestled the Packer fullback to the ground and preserved the NFL championship for the Eagles. "I could see the clock at one corner of Franklin Field," Bednarik recalled. "I wasn't about to move until it ran out, but he started squirming and shouting at me, 'C'mon, you bleepety-bleep, get off me.' But I didn't until that clock hit the zero mark. Then I said, 'Okay, you bleepety-bleep, I'll get up now. You just lost.'"

Linebackers are as likely to hit someone between plays as during one, as Pittsburgh Steelers middle linebacker Jack Lambert showed in Super Bowl X. With Pittsburgh trailing the Dallas Cowboys 10–7 in the third quarter, Steelers kicker Roy Gerela missed a 36-yard field goal. Cowboys free safety Cliff Harris brashly patted Gerela on the helmet and said, "Way to go." Lambert became enraged. He picked up Harris and slammed him to the ground. The Steelers, inspired by Lambert's passion, rallied and won the Super Bowl, 21–17. "When Harris did what he did to Gerela," Lambert said, "I responded the only way I know how. I never want to see us intimidated. Until then, that's exactly what Dallas was doing. It had never happened before while I'd been with the club, and I never want it to happen again. After that we went back to being the Steelers I love and respect."

Great plays by linebackers are not limited to vicious hits. Oakland Raiders weak-side linebacker Rod Martin used his pass coverage skills to help the Raiders defeat the Philadelphia Eagles in Super Bowl XV, 27–10. After intercepting only 2 passes all season, the six-foot-two-inch (191cm), 225-pound (102kg) Martin picked off 3 Ron Jaworski passes to set a Super Bowl record. The interceptions killed several offensive drives by the

ABOVE: **Jack Lambert had a face to match his menacing attitude. Lambert wasn't intimidated by anyone.**

OPPOSITE: **Rod Martin (53) put on a virtual pass coverage clinic in Super Bowl XV. He picked off three passes in the game, a Super Bowl record.**

Eagles and gave the Raiders scoring opportunities, as they converted two of Martin's interceptions into 10 points.

Martin set the tone for the entire Super Bowl when he made his first interception on the Eagles' third play of the game and returned it 16 yards to the Philadelphia 30-yard line. Seven plays later, Oakland scored and never looked back. The interception took the Eagles out of the game mentally. His second interception in the third quarter killed any hopes the Eagles had of coming back. The third pickoff came while the Raiders were in a prevent defense.

It wasn't an accident that Martin had a big game. While some of the fun-loving Raiders were partying on Bourbon Street in New Orleans, Martin watched game films on the projector he kept in his hotel room. He wanted to make sure that he would not be fooled by Jaworski and Eagles wide receiver Harold Carmichael. "I don't know if it was fate, or what," Martin said, "but my sister said two different people told her that I was going to get an interception."

The Raiders got more spectacular pass coverage from another one of their linebackers in Super Bowl XVIII. The Washington Redskins trailed the Raiders

14–3 and had the ball on their own 12-yard line with only 12 seconds remaining in the opening half. Instead of letting the clock run out and going into the locker room still in the game, Redskins head coach Joe Gibbs called a "Rocket Screen" that had gained 63 yards when the two teams met earlier in the season.

Raiders linebacker coach and de facto defensive coordinator Charlie Sumner recognized the offensive formation and hurriedly rushed reserve linebacker Jack Squirek, a pass-defense specialist, into the game in place of Matt Millen, with orders to cover Redskins running back Joe Washington. The Redskins lined up three receivers on the right side and sent them deep as decoys while Washington flared out to his left side. Quarterback Joe Theismann threw a looping pass intended for Washington that the six-foot-four-inch (193m), 235-pound (107kg) Squirek picked off on the run. He coasted into the end zone for a touchdown to put the Raiders firmly in control of the game at the half, 21–3.

"We knew something was up," said Squirek. "[Sumner] told me to play man-for-man with Washington. He said, 'If he catches a pass, don't let him make a large gain. Whatever you do, don't go for the interception, miss the pass, and let him gain a lot of yardage.' Fortunately, I did go for the interception, and everything turned out all right." Indeed, the Redskins never recovered from the blow, and the Raiders went on to win Super Bowl XVIII, 38–9.

Linebackers have also been able to give their teams momentum with textbook tackling. One of the finest examples of tackling came in Super Bowl XVI. The Cincinnati Bengals, trailing the San Francisco 49ers 20–7 late in the third quarter, had a first down at the 49ers' 3-yard line. On first and goal, Pete Johnson, the Bengals' 248-pound (113kg) fullback, smashed through the line of scrimmage behind offensive tackle Anthony Munoz. Defensive tackle John Choma grabbed Johnson by the ankle and reserve linebacker Dan Bunz, who was

two plays away from making the tackle of his life, brought him down at the 1-yard line.

On the next play, the six-foot-four-inch (193cm), 235-pound (107kg) Bunz cut down lead Bengals blocker Charles Alexander, allowing fellow linebacker Jack Reynolds to tackle Johnson for no gain. Next came the critical third-down play. Quarterback Ken Anderson rolled out of the pocket to his right, and Alexander ran in the same direction in front of the goal line. Anderson's pass was slightly behind Alexander, who had to reach back to make the reception. As he caught the ball, Bunz hit him in the chest, wrapped him up, and stopped him cold for no gain.

"That play seemed like a lifetime," Bunz recalled. "I was sprinting toward Alexander and I thought, 'Step forward.' I was right there. It was probably the best you could play it, but I was mad after the tackle. Everyone was screaming and patting me on the back, but I'm thinking that they gained a foot."

The Bengals went for it on fourth down, but the entire 49ers' defense swarmed on top of Johnson to keep the score at 20–7. The 49ers' goal-line stand, inspired by Bunz's one-on-one tackle, turned out to be crucial, as San Francisco won the game 26–21.

The Dallas Cowboys received similar inspiration from linebacker Ken Norton in Super Bowl XXVII. The Cowboys led the Bills 14–7 at the start of the second quarter, but Buffalo had a third and goal from the 1-yard line. The Bills' offensive line bulldozed a lane through the Cowboys' defensive line. Buffalo running back Kenneth Davis charged for the end zone. Norton, however, headed to stop him. He got low for leverage and made a textbook tackle in front of the goal line. The Bills went for it on the fourth down, but Dallas' Thomas Everett intercepted Jim Kelly's pass. The goal-line stand was the turning point in the game. The Bills never recovered, and the Cowboys went on to win the Super Bowl easily, 52–17.

Norton made other big plays in the game. He knocked Kelly out of the game and later scooped up a fumble and raced nine yards for a touchdown. But it was his tackle at the 1-foot line that prevented the Bills from tying the score. "That will always be my dream tackle," Norton said. "When I think about the tackle I want to make, that's it."

Football is a violent sport. The object of the game is to tackle the ballcarrier and prevent him from scoring. After every play, players rise deliberately from a mass of humanity, making sure all body parts are still in working condition. Unfortunately, players are sometimes seriously hurt. Millions of fans watching *Monday Night Football* on November 18, 1985, witnessed a particularly gruesome injury. The New York Giants were visiting the Washington Redskins at Robert F. Kennedy Stadium. With the scored tied at 7–7 early in the second quarter and the ball on the Redskins' 46-yard line, Joe Theismann handed the ball to running back John Riggins. Riggins stopped at the line of scrimmage and pitched the ball back to Theismann for a flea-flicker.

Theismann was supposed to pass, but he never had a chance. The Giants' defense, led by their linebackers, swarmed him. Harry Carson grabbed Theismann first and turned him around. Lawrence Taylor arrived next, hitting him from behind. Finally, Gary Reasons jumped on top and the pile crashed to the turf. As Theismann went down, his lower right leg bent nearly 90 degrees before snapping like a twig.

The players could hear the bone break and see blood on the field. Taylor gestured frantically for the Washington trainers. Theismann had suffered a compound fracture just above the ankle. He would never play football again. The spines of millions of viewers tingled as ABC replayed Theismann's leg bending at a horrific angle. Despite his love of contact and fearsome reputation, Taylor was shaken by the incident: "The idea of this game is to hit a guy hard and make him feel it," said Taylor. "But you don't want to see any kind of major injury or a broken bone. You hate to see something like that."

ABOVE: **Harry Carson and Gary Reasons huddle round Joe Theismann after unintentionally ending his career.**

*OPPOSITE:***Ken Norton (51) knocks Jim Kelly out of Super Bowl XXVII.**

CHAPTER FIVE

THE GREATEST LINEBACKERS OF ALL-TIME

Choosing the best players of a sport is a subjective task. Football, being the consummate team game, poses unique difficulties. Teams implement different defensive schemes, and responsibilities for each position vary from team to team. It's often difficult to determine whether the quarterback who just threw for 400 yards would have done so if his offensive line hadn't given him ample time to find open receivers. Conversely, did the offensive lineman who didn't allow a sack benefit from his quarterback's lightning-quick release?

These questions also apply to linebackers. Responsibilities of linebackers vary not only from team to team but also between inside linebackers and outside linebackers. Nonetheless, there are certain qualities that separate the elite linebackers from the average ones. The best linebackers are versatile enough to play every down. They can stop the run, pressure the quarterback, and cover the pass. The best linebackers are also intelligent. They gain a split-second advantage over their enemies by successfully dissecting offensive formations.

The linebackers gathered here are the best in National Football League history. A profile is provided for each player: from the fierce intensity of the New York Giants' Lawrence Taylor to the unpredictable quirkiness of the Oakland Raiders' Ted Hendricks to the unmatched athletic ability of the San Diego Chargers' Junior Seau. Some of professional football's toughest players, such as the Philadelphia Eagles' Chuck Bednarik, the Chicago Bears' Dick Butkus, and the Green Bay Packers' Ray Nitschke, are also included. Although these men played in different eras and with different styles, they are united by their spectacular play at one of football's most demanding positions.

Junior Seau (55) is a great linebacker because of his versatility. He can run down ballcarriers, cover receivers, and get past blockers to sack quarterbacks.

CHUCK BEDNARIK

Football's last iron man, Chuck Bednarik represents a bygone era of professional football. In 1949, when the Philadelphia Eagles made Bednarik the first overall pick of the NFL draft, it was standard for players to perform regularly on both offense and defense. In some cases, players were on the field for almost the entire sixty minutes of a game, as Bednarik was in the 1960 NFL Championship game.

Not only did Bednarik often play every down, he did so at an all-pro caliber from both sides of the ball. On defense, he preyed on ballcarriers from his linebacker position. On offense, he lined up at center and was an exceptional blocker. Bednarik played in eight Pro Bowl games—six as a linebacker and two as a center—and was named outstanding player of the 1954 contest. This is even more amazing when one considers that he missed only three games during his fourteen-year career and was still playing both ways long after two-way players were replaced by players who specialized on either offense or defense. Bednarik was so versatile that one could debate whether he was enshrined in the Pro Football Hall of Fame in 1967 for his play at linebacker or center. Regardless, Concrete Charlie, as he was called by friend and foe alike, will always be remembered for his bone-jarring tackles.

The son of Slovakian immigrants, Bednarik, raised in the Pennsylvania steel town of Bethlehem and hardened by war, was made to play linebacker in the NFL. A two-time All-American at the University of Pennsylvania, Bednarik was already twenty-four years old when he entered the NFL; service in the military had delayed his professional football debut. The Eagles were the defending NFL champions, but Bednarik stepped into the starting lineup and helped Philadelphia win the championship again in 1949.

Two of the most famous tackles in NFL history defined Bednarik's career. The first occurred in the eighth game of the 1960 season against the New York Giants. The Eagles held a 17–10 lead when Bednarik leveled halfback Frank Gifford, who fumbled the ball and was knocked unconscious. The Eagles recovered the fumble and went on to defeat the Giants, 17–10. Gifford, however, had to be carried off the field on a stretcher. He regained consciousness in the locker room, but he had a fractured skull and intracranial bleeding. The hit forced Gifford to sit out the remainder of the 1960 season and all of 1961.

The second tackle did nothing less than save the 1960 championship for the Eagles. Bednarik had played the entire game and time was running out. While the Eagles were desperately trying to hang on to their 17–13 lead, the Green Bay Packers were driving. In what turned into the final play of the game, the Packers' Jim Taylor caught a pass and headed for the end zone while Bednarik steamrolled to meet him. The two crashed head on at the Eagles' 9-yard line, where Bednarik brought down the powerful fullback to preserve the lead—and the championship—for the Eagles.

The tackle not only brought the game to an end but also closed an era. Bednarik had played for more than fifty-eight minutes in the last two-way performance in NFL history. He played for two more years but never again on both sides of the ball for an entire game. Bednarik remembers the 1960 NFL Championship game with pride: "That day I played fifty-eight and a half minutes at center and left-side linebacker. I did everything but go down on kickoffs. It was the high point of my 14-year career." Bednarik resents talk about players such as Deion Sanders being two-way players. "Don't give me that b.s.," he said. "You've got to play every down." Although the NFL has long since forgotten the two-way player, it has not forgotten Bednarik's performance on the field. In 1994, a Pro Football Hall of Fame committee, organized to celebrate the NFL's seventy-fifth anniversary, named Bednarik to the NFL's All-Decade team of the 1950s.

Chuck Bednarik was talented enouth to play both center and linebacker for the Philadelphia Eagles and be inducted into the Hall of Fame. He played on the Eagles' championship teams of 1949 and 1960.

BOBBY BELL

When football fans think of big, fast, strong, and quick outside linebackers, players such as Lawrence Taylor and Derrick Thomas come to mind. Bobby Bell, however, was the first of the dominating athletes to play outside linebacker. Eventually, Bell's position evolved into that of the dominating pass-rushing linebacker. Players such as Taylor, Thomas, Kevin Greene, Ken Harvey, Greg Lloyd, and Bryce Paup owe a debt to Bell.

At the University of Minnesota, Bell showcased his astonishing versatility by playing such diverse positions as quarterback, tight end, and defensive tackle. In 1962, Bell was an All-American and won the Outland Trophy as the nation's outstanding lineman.

The Kansas City Chiefs of the American Football League (AFL) drafted the six-foot-four-inch (193cm), 230-pound (104kg) Bell in 1963 to play defensive end. When he wasn't playing defense, Bell snapped for field goals and punts. Although Bell was an All-AFL defensive end, Kansas City head coach Hank Stram moved him to left outside linebacker in 1965 to cover speedy running backs on deep routes. It was a perfect match for the athletic Bell, who made the All-AFL/AFC team for the next eight years.

By moving from defensive end to linebacker, Bell gained a split second to diagnose plays. With his quickness, this added time was like an eternity. Bell, who ran the 40-yard dash in 4.5 seconds, had the ability to blanket receivers. He intercepted 26 passes during his career and returned 6 for touchdowns. His total return yardage was 479 for a whopping 18.4 yards average.

Bell was also equally adept at stopping the run. He had the quickness to run down plays from behind and the strength to beat offensive linemen on plays run directly at him. He was an excellent open-field tackler and never allowed the same play to beat him twice. While head coach of the Oakland Raiders John Madden learned that the hard way: "I remember fooling him once with a play-action pass. We faked the run, then the tight end sneaked in behind for the pass. 'Hey, let's try that again,' I told my quarterback. The next time, Bobby Bell stayed with the tight end and knocked down the pass."

Bell's passion for the game also made him a great linebacker. "I just like to play football, but if I had to pick one favorite position, it would be outside linebacker," Bell once said. "It is one of the most challenging positions because you have so many responsibilities. You have to worry about the pass, the run, man-to-man coverage, containing plays, screens, and draws."

With Bell at outside linebacker, the Chiefs played in two Super Bowls, including a 23–7 victory over the Minnesota Vikings in Super Bowl IV. He retired after the 1974 season and in 1983 became the first Kansas City Chief elected to the Pro Football Hall of Fame. In 1994, Bell was named to the NFL's All-Decade team of the 1960s.

Bell was an amazing athlete who could have dominated a game from any position on the football field. At one point during Bell's career, Stram said, "I don't want to get into a discussion about who are my best athletes. I think every man on our team is great, but I will say one thing. If there's a better athlete in football than Bobby Bell, I haven't seen him. You hear a lot about all-round football players, but you don't really see many. There isn't a job Bell couldn't do—and do well."

Bobby Bell was one of the first big, athletic outside linebackers that have become commonplace in the 1990s. Bell's eight career touchdowns reflect his remarkable versatility. Six came on interception returns, one on a fumble recovery, and one came on a kickoff return.

DICK BUTKUS

Some say he was a savage, Cro-Magnon man with a helmet and shoulder pads. Some also say he was the greatest middle linebacker in NFL history. Those who played with or against Dick Butkus all say that he was one incredible player.

Despite already having future Hall of Famer Bill George at middle linebacker, the Bears picked Butkus, a two-time All-American linebacker at the University of Illinois, in the first round of the 1965 NFL draft. The six-foot-three-inch (191cm), 245-pound (111kg) Butkus

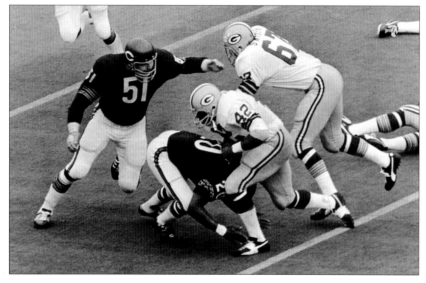

Dick Butkus (51) overcame playing on losing teams to become one of the greatest middle linebackers in NFL history.

beat out the old pro for the starting middle linebacker spot. In his first game, he made 11 unassisted tackles. By the end of his rookie season, Butkus led the Bears in interceptions, fumble recoveries, and tackles, and a legend was born.

What set Butkus apart from other players was his intensity and passion for the physical aspect of the game. "I loved practice, the games, the hitting," he said. "I loved all there was about football. When you put on that uniform, you ought to know what it means, what you're getting into out there. I did, and I loved it."

Butkus also possessed an all-consuming drive to excel. Although he was not the fastest football player—especially at the end of his career when his knees were in bad condition—desire, intelligence, instinct, and intimidation enabled him to bring down a ballcarrier before anyone else. "When I hit a guy," Butkus said, "I wanted him to know who hit him without his ever having to look around and check a number. And I wanted him to know I'd be back. I wanted him to think about me instead of what he was supposed to be doing."

For nine glorious years that philosophy worked flawlessly. Butkus finished his career with 22 interceptions and 25 fumble recoveries, the third-highest total in NFL history, and he played in the Pro Bowl eight years in a row, from 1965 to 1972. These are amazing accomplishments for someone who played for a mediocre team. In 1969, the Bears were 1–13; Butkus, however, was named the NFL Defensive Player of the Year.

Butkus just didn't tackle ballcarriers, he exploded into them. "Sometimes," said former Green Bay Packers guard Jerry Kramer, "it seemed like the guys he was hitting would explode, too." Even though Butkus played linebacker with the viciousness of a hungry animal, he was not simply a hard-driving brute—he was a devoted student of the game. While others played cards on flights to road games, Butkus studied the scouting report of the opponent. He also studied game films—in an era when few players studied film—to look for the slightest advantage.

Although he expressed a desire to keep playing football until he was sixty years old, knee surgery in 1971 to repair loose ligaments marked the beginning of the end of Butkus' career. By the end of the 1973 season, Butkus' injured knees had worsened and forced him to hang up his cleats. He was never able to find another

pursuit to satisfy his ferocious appetite for the game. "What I miss is the violence," Butkus said. "Life is very boring to me now."

In 1979, Butkus was elected to the Pro Football Hall of Fame. In 1994, a Pro Football Hall of Fame committee, organized to celebrate the NFL's seventy-fifth anniversary, named him to the NFL's All-Time team, a collection of the 48 greatest players in NFL history. Despite playing for only nine years, Butkus left a mark on the NFL that was as big as the bruises he inflicted on running backs. Former Bears center Mike Pyle, a teammate of Butkus, said, "I'm one of the people who think Dick Butkus was, without question, the best middle linebacker who ever played."

Dick Butkus (51) always played with intensity and ferociousness, even in this 1969 Armed Forces Benefit game.

BILL GEORGE

In the modern world of professional football, it's hard to imagine an All-American defensive tackle entering the NFL, playing for a couple of years on the defensive line, and then moving to middle linebacker. That is, however, exactly what Bill George did with the Chicago Bears in the 1950s.

When George, a six-foot-two-inch (188cm), 230-pound (104kg) All-American tackle from Wake Forest College, joined the Bears in 1952, the standard professional defensive alignment consisted of five defensive linemen, two linebackers, and four defensive backs. On passing plays, the middle guard bumped the center before dropping back into pass coverage. The Bears put George at the middle guard position, where he earned All-Pro honors in 1952 and 1953.

In a game against the Philadelphia Eagles in 1954, however, George was regularly getting beaten on passing plays. Instead of first bumping the center, George immediately stood up and took a step off the line of scrimmage. On the first play, he knocked down the pass. On the second play, George recorded the first of his 18 career interceptions. The position of middle linebacker was born, and NFL defenses were changed forever. By 1957, the position of middle linebacker replaced middle guard on the All-Pro team.

Some football historians debate whether George was truly the first middle linebacker, but no one can debate that he was the first to play that position regularly. He was also one of the best who ever played the position, as his appearance in eight Pro Bowls in a row—from 1955 to 1962—attests. George was also instrumental in making the middle linebacker the field general of the defense. The Bears had hundreds of defensive alignments. In 1956, George was given the responsibility of learning all the defensive variations and making them work on the field. Since then, almost every team in the NFL has used the middle linebacker to call its defensive signals.

George was a strong, intelligent, aggressive player who believed in the blitz. "You've got to put pressure on the good quarterbacks," he said. "Once we went into a three-man line with eight players in the secondary to face Johnny Unitas, and he picked us to pieces. You just can't let the good quarterbacks get set."

George's skill with the blitz helped to quell the San Francisco 49ers' powerful offense of the early 1960s. San Francisco used a version of the shotgun formation to give receivers more time to get open downfield. George simply moved closer to the line of scrimmage, blew by the center at the snap, and got to the quarterback almost as quickly as the ball. Other teams learned from George's wisdom, and the 49ers had to abandon their once-terrorizing formation.

Stepping off the line of scrimmage and blitzing to stop the pass are prime examples of George's intelligence. George Allen, who coached the player in Chicago and Los Angeles, said, "Bill George was the smartest defensive player I ever coached. He called defensive signals for the Bears when they were at their best defensively. He made as few mistakes as any player I've seen."

A well-rounded player, George was also strong against the run. He stuffed the middle, and, having wrestled at Wake Forest, when he tackled ballcarriers they went down and didn't get away. With George patrolling the middle, the Bears played in two NFL Championship games, including their 14–10 victory over the New York Giants in 1963. After 14 seasons with the Bears, George played with the Los Angeles Rams for one season before retiring in 1966. In 1974, he was elected to the Pro Football Hall of Fame. In 1994, George was named to the NFL's All-Decade team of the 1950s.

As the first true middle linebacker, Bill George was an innovator on defense. George also helped make the middle linebacker the defensive leader.

JACK HAM

To Jack Ham, football was a science and the football field was his laboratory. Perhaps no one in NFL history played outside linebacker, with all its required techniques and responsibilities, better than Ham, who used exceptional speed and a superior diagnostic ability to make plays.

When the Pittsburgh Steelers drafted the All-American from Penn State in 1971, they were looking for someone who could make the big plays. In Ham they found one who specialized in making big plays in big games. During his twelve-year career, Ham intercepted 32 passes (the most among Hall of Fame linebackers) and recovered 19 fumbles. In the 1974 season, he intercepted 5 passes. Ham, however, didn't like being labeled a big-play player. "I prefer to play consistent, error-free football," he said.

Ham's greatest single-game performance probably came in the 1974 AFC Championship game against the Oakland Raiders. In that game, Ham made 2 interceptions in the fourth quarter to help the Steelers advance to the first of four Super Bowls in the 1970s. For his career, Ham intercepted 2 passes in a single game on four seperate occasions. Perhaps it was Ham's scientific, cold-blooded style that allowed him to perform so well under pressure.

"We were sitting on the bench during a game, and [Ham] was telling me about some stock deal he was interested in," recalled Andy Russell, the right outside linebacker who played opposite Ham. "Then we had to go out on defense. On the first play, Jack read the pass and took a perfect drop, deflected the ball with one hand, caught it with the other, got tackled, flipped the ball to the ref, and overtook me on the way off the field. 'Like I was telling you, it's a really good investment,' he said, like nothing at all had happened."

The six-foot-one-inch (185m), 220-pound (100kg) Ham was the prototype outside linebacker. "Of all the outside linebackers I coached against, he was the best," said John Madden. "He had the best feet, the best footwork. He was never out of position. If you tried to run inside, he could close down on the ballcarrier. If you tried to run outside, he could string it out and stop it. If you tried to pass against a zone, he could get back to his zone. If you tried to pass against man-to-man coverage, he could cover his man."

Although most linebackers would acknowlege that they live to knock off a ballcarrier's head, Ham enjoyed his pass defense responsibilities the most. "I love playing pass coverage," Ham said. "Some people think of a linebacker only as a guy who can get to the right hole in a hurry and hit hard. To me, that's less than half of being

a linebacker. You've got to do your job on pass coverage, or else you're a liability."

Although he was quiet and unassuming, Ham's talent did not go unnoticed by his peers. He played in eight consecutive Pro Bowls—from 1973 to 1980—and was named the NFL Defensive Player of the Year in 1975. Of course, Ham was an integral member of the Steelers' four championship teams of the 1970s.

A dislocated toe sidelined Ham for the Steelers' final Super Bowl victory in 1980. He never completely recovered from the injury, and after the 1982 season, he retired. He closed his career with his typical impartial analysis: "The films don't lie," he said "There has been a drop off." In 1988, he was elected to the Pro Football Hall of Fame. In 1994, he was named to the NFL's All-Time team.

ABOVE: **Jack Ham's deftness in pass coverage made him one of football's all-time great outside linebackers.**

OPPOSITE: **Jack Ham (59) preferred the analytical side of football, but he could still deliver the big hit, as he does here on Cleveland fullback Mike Pruitt. Ham's speed, mobility, and intelligence made him the prototypical outside linebacker.**

T E D   H E N D R I C K S

Typical football players do not usually arrive at practice by riding a horse to the middle of the field, as Ted Hendricks once did while playing for the Oakland Raiders. Then again, Hendricks was never what you would call a typical athlete.

In addition to his free-wheeling spirit, the most striking characteristic of Hendricks was his six-foot-seven-inch (201cm), 235-pound (107kg) frame. Although his size helped to make him one of the most dominating outside linebackers in NFL history, pro scouts initially wondered where to play the Mad Stork, as Hendricks was known because of the way he thrashed his arms about wildly. A three-time All-American defensive end at the University of Miami, Hendricks seemed too light to play defensive end and too tall to play linebacker in the NFL. In what they considered a gamble, the Baltimore Colts selected Hendricks in the second round of the 1969 NFL draft.

Hendricks played mostly on special teams during his initial seasons in the league, but before long he was the starting right outside linebacker. Hendricks helped the Colts win Super Bowl V, but his off-field antics disturbed the Colts' conservative management. In 1974, the Colts traded him to the Green Bay Packers. The next year, when Hendricks was a free agent, the Oakland Raiders gladly gave the Packers two first-round picks for the rights to sign the Pro Bowl linebacker. Hendricks fit in perfectly with the fast-living, hard-playing Raiders—and flourished. "Everywhere I've been," Hendricks said when he joined the Raiders, "I've been the screwball on the team—in college, with the Colts, with the Packers—but here I'm just a normal guy."

Making the most of his height, Hendricks became an extraordinary blitzer, pass defender, and run stopper. He could swat down passes in a zone as easily as he could cover the tight end man-to-man. His strength, quickness, and lateral mobility allowed him to stop running backs trying to get outside to the right.

The clothesline was a legal hit for part of Hendricks's career. With a size 37 sleeve, Hendricks made it his trademark. Hendricks's long arms enabled him to level quarterbacks and running backs and to recover fumbles. For his career, he picked off 26 passes and recovered 16 fumbles. He was also a great kick blocker, recording an unofficial NFL career-record 25 blocks of field goals, extra points, and punts. But what Hendricks did best of all was freelance, using his uncanny ability to diagnose plays.

The Raiders quickly recognized that Hendricks was a maverick, and they let him play accordingly. He floated around the line of scrimmage, blitzed when appropriate, or dropped back into pass coverage. Offenses never knew what he was going to do. As a result, they had a difficult time neutralizing him. "Any offensive game plan against Oakland," George Allen said," should start with neutralizing Hendricks as much as possible. That's the mark of a great player—that he requires special handling."

John Madden, who coached the warm-hearted Hendricks for four years, once joked, "Ted's elevator doesn't go all the way to the top." There's no denying, however, that Hendricks was one of the top linebackers of all time. Throughout his fifteen-year career, Hendricks never missed a game, proving that his gangly physique was not a liability. Hendricks's four career safeties tied an NFL record. He played in eight Pro Bowls and won four Super Bowls, balancing personal honor with team success.

Hendricks retired after the Los Angeles Raiders won Super Bowl XVIII in 1984. He let it be known that he didn't appreciate those who questioned his height and weight. "They didn't think I could play linebacker at my weight," Hendricks said. "Well, that is really quite silly. If you're good, you're good." In 1990, he was elected to the Pro Football Hall of Fame. In 1994, Hendricks was named to the NFL's All-Time team.

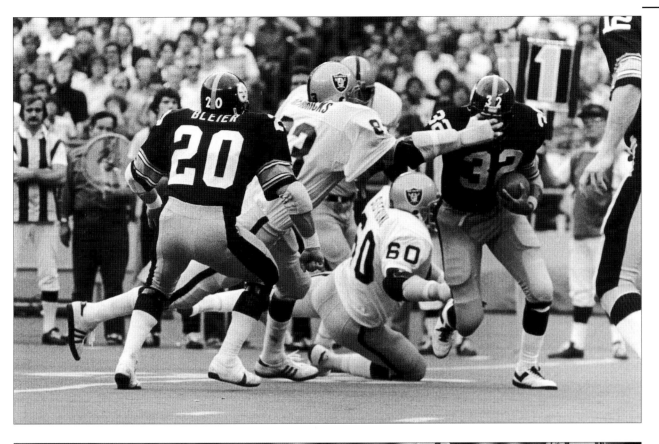

TOP: Ted Hendricks (83) personified the Oakland Raiders' intimidating style of play.

BOTTOM: Sacks weren't an official statistic during most of Ted Hendricks's career, but he was an excellent pass rusher. Here, Hendricks zeroes in on Steve Grogan.

SAM HUFF

Sam Huff was professional football's first acclaimed defensive player. Some argue that the media exposure that came with playing for the New York Giants brought him undeserved notoriety. Others believe that Huff's battles with the great Jim Brown brought him into focus. Both of these factors probably contributed to Huff's fame, but, regardless of press, he still had to hold up his end of the bargain and perform well, which he did every Sunday for thirteen seasons.

An All-American defensive lineman at West Virginia University, Huff was a third-round draft pick of the New York Giants in 1956. Head coach Jim Lee Howell couldn't decide where to play the six-foot-one-inch (185cm), 230-pound (104kg) rookie. Discouraged, Huff walked out of training camp, but Giants assistant coach Vince Lombardi coaxed him to stay. As fate would have it, Huff got a chance to play when middle linebacker Ray Beck went down with an injury. Soon professional football had a new hero.

Combining power, speed, and intelligence, Huff anchored the strong Giants defenses of the late 1950s and early 1960s. He was a hard hitter who flourished in defensive coordinator Tom Landry's four-three defense, which used the middle linebacker to recognize and react to the unfolding play. Besides his run-stopping abilities, Huff could also defend the pass. His recording of 30 career interceptions is the second highest among Hall of Fame linebackers.

Huff wasn't content with simply tackling a ballcarrier; he liked to intimidate his opponents. "We didn't get paid to look fancy," Huff said. "The idea was to stop the runner the best way you could. Sometimes I twisted their heads a little, but most of them didn't seem to mind. Football is a man's game, and any guy who doesn't want to hit hard doesn't belong in it."

In the 1950s and 1960s, New York and the Cleveland Browns competed for the Eastern Conference title nearly every year, and Huff's fierce confrontations with Jim Brown became legendary. Although his nose was broken and two of his teeth were knocked out in one collision with Brown, Huff and the Giants enjoyed much success against the powerful fullback. In a five-game stretch during the late 1950s, Brown gained no more than 50 yards a game against Huff and the Giants. In 1958, the Browns and Giants finished the season in a tie for first place. In the ensuing playoff game, Brown gained just eight yards on seven carries and the Giants won the game.

Success, both his own and that of his team, and playing in New York brought Huff much media exposure and notoriety. In 1959 he appeared on the cover of *Time* magazine. The following year, he was the subject of a CBS documentary entitled "The Violent World of Sam Huff." Huff believes that all the attention he received created resentment that hurt him during his career and delayed his election to the Pro Football Hall of Fame until 1982, eight years after he was eligible for enshrinement. "In 1959, I was named defensive MVP of the NFL," said Huff. "In 1960, after 'The Violent World of Sam Huff,' I didn't even make all-pro, and I had a better year in 1960 than I'd had in 1959. It is the only thing I can think of that kept me [from making] the Hall of Fame in five years. All the guys I was compared to and who were compared to me—Joe Schmidt, Bill George—made it in five."

In 1964, Huff was traded to the Washington Redskins. He retired after the 1967 season but returned to the Redskins in 1969 as a player-coach under Vince Lombardi. During his eight years in New York, the Giants appeared in six NFL Championship games, winning the 1956 title contest, and Huff played in four Pro Bowls. In 1994, Huff was named to the NFL's All-Decade team of the 1950s. As for the criticism that he was overrated, George Allen, who coached against Huff, said, "[Huff] deserved all the attention he attracted, and he earned the Hall of Fame selection he got in 1982."

Sam Huff's personality and talent made middle linebacker a glamorous position, as did his perennial duels with Jim Brown.

JACK LAMBERT

All NFL players are gladiators, but no one personified that role more than Jack Lambert. With his savage snarl, which looked even more menacing because of three missing front teeth, and his feet pumping up and down furiously before the snap of the ball, as if calling the gods to accompany him into battle, quarterbacks must have been thankful that football is not a fight to the death.

At six feet four inches (193cm) and 220 pounds (100kg), pro scouts considered Lambert too tall and too light to play middle linebacker. The Pittsburgh Steelers, however, liked Lambert's athleticism and drafted him out of Kent State in the second round of the 1974 NFL draft. Because of a strike by veteran players in the early days of the 1974 training camp and injuries to starting middle linebacker Harry Davis, Lambert got a chance to play and made the most of it. He proved to be the final component in the construction of the "Steel Curtain" defense that led Pittsburgh to four Super Bowl victories in six years.

The 1974 NFL Defensive Rookie of the Year, Lambert possessed all the physical talents of a great linebacker. Quickness enabled him to get to a ballcarrier before anyone else, and when he arrived, he could deliver a vicious blow. Lambert led the Steelers in tackles for ten straight seasons between 1974 and 1983. Speed allowed him to be an exceptional defender against the pass. During his eleven-year career, Lambert intercepted 28 passes and recovered 15 fumbles. His 7 recoveries of opponent's fumbles in 1976 is the third-highest season total in NFL history. In 1979, Lambert's 6 interceptions were the most among NFL linebackers. He also had the intangible qualities of a great linebacker. He had great instinct and was a leader who constantly exhorted his teammates to excellence.

Teammates and opponents alike recognized Lambert's mastery at middle linebacker. He played in nine consecutive Pro Bowls—from 1975 to 1983—and was the NFL Defensive Player of the Year in 1976 and 1979. "Lambert was as good as any of the great linebackers against the run, but he was dramatically better than any of them against the pass," said former Steelers linebacker Andy Russell, a teammate of Lambert. "They put him into coverage 30 yards downfield. He called the defensive signals. He set the tone. He was intelligent, all business, a terrific leader."

A quiet, soft-spoken man off the field, Lambert will always be remembered for his intensity on the gridiron. One play in particular symbolized his passion for the game and his loyalty to his teammates. With the Dallas Cowboys ahead 10–7 in the third quarter of Super Bowl X, Steelers kicker Roy Gerela missed a 36-yard field goal. Cowboys free safety Cliff Harris taunted Gerela by patting him on the helmet and saying, "Way to go." Lambert rushed to his teammate's defense and flung Harris to the ground like a rag doll. The Steelers rallied around their leader and won, 21–17. After the game, Steelers head coach Chuck Noll said, "Jack Lambert is a defender of what is right."

Although Lambert missed just six games because of injury in his first ten years, a severely dislocated toe in the first game in 1984 forced him to retire after that season. In 1990, Lambert was elected to the Pro Football Hall of Fame. In 1994, he was named to the NFL's All-Time team.

Former Steelers president Art Rooney recognized Lambert's contribution to the Steelers and the NFL when he said, "Jack Lambert demanded total effort from everybody in the organization. He took us to greatness. He was the symbol of our success in the 1970s."

Jack Lambert (58) anchored the Steelers' defense that led Pittsburgh to four Super Bowl victories.

WILLIE LANIER

Known to his teammates as "Contact" or "Bear" because of his fierce play, Willie Lanier hit so hard that he suffered a series of concussions early in his career. This required him to wear a specially padded helmet to protect his head from further trauma. During his eleven-year career, however, Lanier never stopped attacking ballcarriers with fearless abandon.

Willie Lanier (63) corrals the elusive O.J. Simpson.

The Kansas City Chiefs picked Lanier, a Little All-American at Morgan State, in the second round of the 1967 AFL draft. By the fourth game of his rookie season, the six-foot-one-inch (185cm), 245-pound (111kg) Lanier was the Chiefs' starting middle linebacker. Size and strength made him difficult to block on running plays, and speed and quickness allowed him to cover receivers on passing plays. He recorded 27 pass interceptions and 15 fumble recoveries in his career. Lanier's intelligence and analytical abilities, however, are what separated him from the average middle linebacker. "It's not easy running against a grizzly bear," said former Miami Dolphins running back Larry Csonka. "But Willie goes one step further. He's a smart grizzly bear."

Despite his excellent play, Lanier didn't receive as much public recognition as some other middle linebackers. Football fans and insiders, however, recognized his talent. "You hear a lot about Dick Butkus and [Atlanta's] Tommy Nobis," Dallas Cowboys assistant coach Ermel Allen once commented, "but Willie Lanier is really the best middle linebacker in pro football."

With Lanier anchoring the Chiefs' defense, Kansas City won Super Bowl IV with a 23–7 victory over the Minnesota Vikings. In a playoff game prior to the Super Bowl, Lanier had given the performance that defined his career. The Chiefs were clinging to a 6–3 lead over the New York Jets in the fourth quarter. The Jets, however, had the ball, first and goal on Kansas City's 1-yard line. At that moment, Lanier's emotions took over. "Willie became almost hysterical. He was crying and screaming," said former Chiefs cornerback Emmitt Thomas. "When the Jets came up to the line, Willie yelled, 'Dammit, they're not going to score on us!' Next thing we knew, we all were saying it and we just kept saying it, over and over." The Chiefs rallied around Lanier. They stuffed two runs and stopped Joe Namath's third-down pass. The Jets managed a field goal, but the Chiefs held on to win 13–6.

After the Chiefs' Super Bowl victory, Lanier started to get some of the credit he deserved. In 1970, the NFL Players Association named him the outstanding linebacker of the NFL. Lanier recognized that he was professional football's first outstanding black middle linebacker. "I was well aware that there had never been a

Willie Lanier (63) was the first African-American football player to become a top middle linebacker. Here, he chases quarterback Mike Rae.

black starting middle linebacker," Lanier said. "Maybe that made me work a little harder, I don't know. I just wanted to play pro ball and play the best way I could."

Lanier combined physical prowess with intelligence in a way that few middle linebackers have equaled. "Playing middle linebacker is sort of a science," Lanier said. "It involves mathematics, geometry, and angles.

There is great joy in exploding into a man, but you can not do that on every play. You must learn to control your aggressiveness."

After playing in eight Pro Bowls, Lanier retired following the 1977 season. In 1986, he was elected to the Pro Football Hall of Fame. In 1994, he was named to the NFL's All-Time team.

R A Y   N I T S C H K E

Ray Nitschke's off-field demeanor contrasted vividly with his on-field image. Off the field, with his horn-rimmed glasses and conservative business attire, Nitschke was a paragon of politeness and consideration. On the football field, with his blood-stained and muddied uniform and his body wrapped in tape to protect his battle scars, this respectable citizen metamorphosed into a ferocious, hard-hitting middle linebacker.

Before he became a success in professional football, however, Nitschke overcame much personal adversity. His father died when Nitschke was a young child, and his mother died when he was thirteen years old. Nitschke was raised by his older brother. Somewhat bitter, Nitschke became a neighborhood bully who eventually found sports as a viable outlet for his frustrations. He was an excellent high school athlete and could have played college football or professional baseball. He chose the former.

A fullback and linebacker at the University of Illinois, the six-foot-three-inch (191cm), 240-pound (109kg) Nitschke was selected by the Packers in the third round of the 1957 NFL draft. Once he worked his way into the starting lineup, Nitschke became the prototype middle linebacker, an extension of Packers head coach Vince Lombardi on the field; he was strong, tough, passionate, and intelligent. "He seems incapable of letting up, even against his own teammates," former Packers guard Jerry Kramer once said. "He's always grabbing people, hitting people, throwing elbows."

Nitschke's strength and lateral mobility aided him immensely in stopping the run. When offensive linemen tried to block him, Nitschke often struck with a forearm that knocked them to the ground. Nitschke's speed and agility made him a superior pass defender. In his fifteen-year career, he intercepted 25 passes and recovered 20 fumbles. He credited most of his success to Lombardi. "The guy never let up," Nitschke said. "But he was consistent. And I knew he was good for me. He wanted me not only to be a good player but to be a good guy."

Nitschke will be remembered best for his savage tackling. Former Bears running back Ronnie Bull said Nitschke hit him the hardest he had ever been hit. It was Bull's rookie year, and he was running an end around. Just as he went to make his cut, Nitschke hit him. "I never saw him," Bull said. "And I got up looking for a truck."

Nitschke will also be remembered as a winner. Between 1960 and 1965, the Green Bay Packers played in four NFL Championship games and won three of them. In 1966 and 1967, the Packers won the first two Super Bowls. Nitschke was at the heart of those championship defenses. He was voted the most valuable player of the 1962 NFL Championship game in which the Packers defeated the New York Giants, 16–7. In that game, he deflected a pass for an interception and recovered 2 fumbles.

Unbelievably, the five-time NFL champion was elected to only one Pro Bowl appearance in his brilliant career. The Packers had a number of talented players, and Nitschke always seemed to be overlooked. He did, however, manage to get some recognition from his peers. In 1967, the NFL Players Association named Nitschke the most outstanding linebacker of the NFL. He retired after the 1972 season. In retirement, Nitschke has received recognition commensurate with his level of play. In 1978, he was elected to the Pro Football Hall of Fame, and in 1994, he was named to the NFL's All-Time team.

Even though his feats were often ignored by his contemporaries, Nitschke was not fazed—he was more interested in playing aggressive, fundamentally sound football than obtaining personal glory. "You want them to respect you when they run a play," he said. "You want them to remember that you are there."

Preparation allowed Ray Nitschke (66) to be a leader on the field. A fierce tackler, he was the middle linebacker on five NFL championship teams.

JOE SCHMIDT

As a member of the Detroit Lions from 1953 through 1965, Joe Schmidt epitomized the role of middle linebacker as quarterback of the defense. He diligently studied the opposition's offensive formations so that he was always ready to call a counterplay. With his love of the analytical side of football, it's not surprising that Schmidt took over as head coach of the Lions in 1967 and compiled an overall record of 43–35–7 during his six-year tenure. Schmidt, however, made his true mark on the NFL through his intelligent play at middle linebacker: "Schmidt played his position perfectly and called defensive signals brilliantly," said former Los Angeles Rams and Washington Redskins head coach George Allen. "He studied his opponents and diagnosed plays as well as anyone ever did. He was always on the runner and seldom missed a tackle or made a mistake."

Because Schmidt was often injured at the University of Pittsburgh, professional scouts were wary of drafting him. Lions assistant coach Buster Ramsey, however, liked what he saw of Schmidt at the Senior Bowl. The Lions selected the All-American in the seventh round of the 1953 NFL draft, but Schmidt's arrival at training camp was treated with indifference.

The Lions were the defending NFL champions, and Schmidt did little more than sit on the bench at the start of the season. When a starting linebacker went down with an injury, however, Schmidt got his chance to play. He made the most of this opportunity and never came out of the starting lineup. The Lions went on to win the 1953 NFL Championship game but lost the 1954 title game. After the team fell to last place in 1955, head coach Buddy Parker decided to change his defense from the traditional five-two set to the new four-three formation being used by some teams. Schmidt moved to middle linebacker and immediately became one of the best in the game.

Although Schmidt was relatively small at six feet (183cm) and 220 pounds (100kg), strength, agility, and sure tackling allowed him to evade blockers and bring down ballcarriers. Speed and intelligence enabled him to cover receivers. In his thirteen-year career, Schmidt recorded 24 interceptions. His 8 recoveries of opponent's fumbles in 1955 is the second-highest season total in NFL history.

Schmidt's most important quality may have been his ability to diagnose plays in a split second before making the defensive call. "He's a great tackler and a strong leader," Vince Lombardi once said, "and he can diagnose a play in an instant."

One of Schmidt's favorite tactics was to send his linebackers through gaps in the line of scrimmage to web running backs and quarterbacks in the backfield, a strategy known as "red dogging." "I'd say about 75 percent of our defensive rushes include some kind of red dog," Schmidt once said. "It confuses the offense and keeps them off balance."

A natural devotion to the game also made Schmidt a great linebacker. "I dearly loved to play football," he said. "To me, it was a privilege and an honor to play in the National Football League."

With Schmidt leading the defense, the Lions won another NFL championship in 1957. Schmidt was selected to play in the Pro Bowl for ten years running—from 1955 to 1964—before he retired after the 1965 season. In 1973, he was elected to the Pro Football Hall of Fame. In 1994, Schmidt was named to the NFL's All-Decade team of the 1950s.

Schmidt helped mold the role of middle linebacker into the most important defensive position in the game. Parker paid Schmidt the ultimate compliment when he said, "His style of play brought about the zone defense, revolving defenses, and the modern defensive look of pro football."

Although he is not as glorified as Dick Butkus, Ray Nitschke, or Sam Huff, Joe Schmidt (56) was instrumental in making middle linebacker the most important defensive position.

JUNIOR SEAU

Modern professional football is a game of specialization. Few linebackers play on running downs and passing downs, and fewer still can play middle linebacker and outside linebacker. However, Junior Seau is one of the rare athletes who can do it all.

At the University of Southern California, the six-foot-three-inch (191cm), 255-pound (116kg) Seau was the nation's best pass-rushing outside linebacker. An All-American his junior year, Seau decided to forego his senior year and enter the NFL draft. The San Diego

Chargers snatched him in the first round of the 1990 college draft.

Although Seau had played outside linebacker at USC, San Diego head coach Bobby Ross moved him to middle linebacker during his rookie season. Seau was not happy with the move. "I didn't know anything else but the outside linebacker position," he said. "All I knew was blitz." With dedication and hard work, however, Seau has blossomed into the NFL's top middle linebacker. In 1992, *Football Digest* named him the NFL Defensive Player of the Year.

A rare combination of size, speed, and quickness allows Seau to take on blockers, run down ballcarriers, cover receivers, and sack quarterbacks. In his seven-year career, Seau has totaled 6 interceptions, 8 fumble recoveries, and 20 sacks. Seau has recorded at least 100 tackles every year except his rookie season. "Junior Seau is the best defensive player we've faced by a pretty good margin," said former Cleveland Browns head coach Bill Belichick. "He does it all. He can play at the point of attack, he chases down plays, he plays the run, he plays the pass. He's a guy nobody's really been able to stop."

Like all great linebackers, intensity and desire complement Seau's physical talents. Two plays into his first NFL game, Seau was ejected. He never gives up on a play. In a 1991 game against the Los Angeles Raiders, Seau came from behind to catch wide receiver Sam Graddy, a gold medalist in the 4 × 100 meter relay race and a silver medalist in the 100-meter race of the 1984 Olympic games. In a 1992 game against the Kansas City Chiefs, Seau allowed a pass completion that allowed the Chiefs to kick the game-winning field goal. The next day, he felt compelled to address the team. "It'll never happen again," Seau said, with tears streaming down his face. He stopped sobbing only after being consoled by his teammates.

During the second half of the 1994 season and the entire postseason, he played with a pinched nerve that caused occasional numbness in his left shoulder and arm. Still Seau led the Chargers to a berth in Super Bowl XXIX. "Yes, I have the injuries," he said before the Super Bowl. "But you still have to go out there on the field and perform the way you are expected to, the way you expect to. I'm not going to help this team by not being out there performing."

One criticism leveled against Seau is that he sometimes plays out of control. Seau's supporters, however, counter that he disrupts and confuses the offense. "He plays within the [defensive] scheme, and then goes beyond it, which not many people can do," explained Bill Arnsparger, then San Diego's defensive coordinator, prior to Super Bowl XXIX. "It's because of his ability to run. Say he has a gap responsibility; if that gap isn't attacked, then his responsibility becomes a very large area. It might give the impression that he's freelancing, but he's not."

NFL players recognize Seau's greatness. He has played in six Pro Bowls in a row and was named NFL's outstanding linebacker by the NFL Players Association in 1993 and 1994. In 1994, Seau was named to the NFL's All-Decade team of the 1990s. "They talk about Lawrence Taylor and Mike Singletary," said former defensive end Greg Townsend, "but he's like both of them put into one."

ABOVE: **Junior Seau's athleticism makes him the top middle linebacker in the game today. He helped the San Diego Chargers to the AFC Championship in 1994.**

OPPOSITE: **Intensity and toughness define the play of Junior Seau.**

MIKE SINGLETARY

"To me, playing middle linebacker is like war," Mike Singletary once said. It was a perfect analogy, for Singletary was one of the best field generals in NFL history. On every play, he scanned the enemy's offense with his protruding eyes, barked the defensive alignments, and then threw his body violently into the pile of human wreckage on the line of scrimmage. A throwback to the old days of the NFL, Singletary carried on the tradition of the emotional, instinctive, and intelligent middle linebacker.

An All-American and the Southwest Conference Player of the Year during his last two seasons at Baylor University, Singletary was selected by the Chicago Bears in the second round of the 1981 NFL draft. In his four years at Baylor, Singletary broke his helmet on 16 different occasions, a far cry from the two or three typically broken by the entire team each year. The six-foot (183cm), 230-pound (104kg) Singletary brought his big hits to Chicago and was soon dubbed "Samurai" because of the war cry he bellowed when making a tackle. He dedicated himself to becoming the best linebacker in the NFL. Singletary constantly asked Bears defensive coordinator Buddy Ryan what he had to do to get better.

As Singletary was learning the professional game, Ryan was perfecting his famous "46" defense. Complicated and technical, the "46" defense required an intelligent middle linebacker to read the offense and make the appropriate defensive call. Singletary was also required to blitz, stop the run, and cover receivers. Preparation became Singletary's trademark. He studied game plans and watched films tirelessly. Soon he developed into one of the finest middle linebackers in NFL history. "He had great intensity and leadership ability," said Ryan. "He was tough, smart, and a great tackler. He could cover people all over the field. He had everything except height."

Although Singletary recorded relatively few career interceptions and sacks, his textbook tackling, intelli-gence, and leadership helped to turn the Bears defense into one of the greatest of all time. An unparalleled run stopper, Singletary tallied at least 100 tackles for each of ten consecutive seasons. Singletary's preparation and talent for diagnosing plays allowed him to change defensive fronts as soon as the offense changed its formation. "Sometimes I felt Mike knew our plays better than some guys in my huddle," said former Detroit Lions quarterback Eric Hipple. "You could hear him calling out gaps that we were going to run through. I would audible and he would counter. I believe he'd bait me, just to have me change the play so he could get me to run something he wanted."

In 1984 and 1985, the Bears had the number-one ranked defense in the NFL. Singletary was the hub of the 1985 defense that was arguably the best in pro football history. Led by the defense, the Bears won Super Bowl XX after the 1985 season. "Mike is the glue that holds this defense together," said former Bears linebacker Otis Wilson.

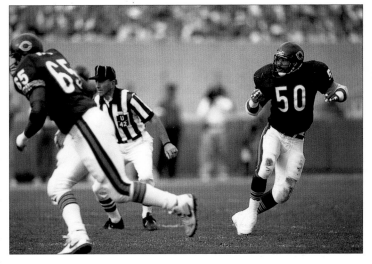

The NFL Defensive Player of the Year in 1985 and 1988, Singletary missed only 2 games during his 12-year career, and he played in ten consecutive Pro Bowls—from 1983 to 1992—before retiring after the 1992 season. In 1994, Singletary was named to the NFL's All-Decade team of the 1980s. "He should make the Hall of Fame," said former Cleveland Browns general manager Ernie Accorsi. "He was the best of his era at his position, the focal point of a championship team. Those are pretty strong credentials."

ABOVE: **Mike Singletary (50) was the NFL Defensive Player of the Year in 1985. That year, the Chicago Bears went 15–1 and won Super Bowl XX.**

OPPOSITE: **With his concentration and analytical ability, Mike Singletary (50) was like a coach on the field.**

LAWRENCE TAYLOR

On the football field, Lawrence Taylor was more powerful than Superman. Although Superman's adversaries could use kryptonite to debilitate him, offensive linemen, tight ends, and running backs could only band together to try to stop Taylor from demolishing ballcarriers and quarterbacks. If not the greatest defensive player in NFL history, Taylor was easily the league's greatest pass-rushing linebacker.

The New York Giants made the All-American outside linebacker from the University of North Carolina the second overall selection in the 1981 NFL draft. It didn't take long for Taylor to make his presence felt. Lining up on the weak side of the Giants three-four defense, Taylor recorded 94 unassisted tackles and 9.5 sacks in his rookie season. The Giants made the playoffs, and Taylor was named the NFL Rookie of the Year and the NFL Defensive Player of the Year.

Building around Taylor, who in 1982 was again named the NFL Defensive Player of the Year, the Giants continued to improve. By the mid 1980s, they were ready to contend for the National Football Conference title. Taylor's finest year in the NFL was 1986. He recorded 20.5 sacks, the fourth-highest total for a single season, and won the NFL's Most Valuable Player award. That same year, Taylor led the Giants to victory in Super Bowl XXI.

Between 1981, his rookie year, and 1993, when he retired, Taylor recorded 132.5 sacks, the second-highest total in NFL history at the time. Because he relished splattering quarterbacks, no one was feared more than Taylor. "There's a sack, and then, there's a *sack*," Taylor said. "You run up behind the quarterback. He doesn't see you. You put your helmet in his back, wrap yourself around him, throw him to the ground, and then the coach comes running out and asks, 'Are you all right?'"

Taylor's aggressive play had an incredible impact on his team and the NFL. The Giants played defense like

a school of sharks in a feeding frenzy, and Taylor was the Great White in perpetual search of prey. He was everywhere on the field doing whatever was necessary to make a play. "Jumping and diving into people," Taylor said, "making everyone else around me crazy too." Opponents had to design their offensive game plans around Taylor. "He was a great football player," said former Philadelphia Eagles head coach Buddy Ryan. "If you were going to beat the New York Giants you had to block Lawrence Taylor. If you didn't do that, all your other scenarios didn't make any difference."

On a wider scale, Taylor's thirteen-year career redefined the position of outside linebacker. More and more NFL teams made the switch to the three-four defense and looked for an athletic outside linebacker with the power to sack quarterbacks and the speed to cover receivers. Thus, because of Taylor, many of the best athletes in professional football today are outside linebackers. "Years ago in college," said former New York Giants head coach Bill Parcells, "LT would have

been playing offense. They took guys like Lawrence who could really run and made them fullbacks and tight ends. Now, in college, almost all the big and fast guys are on defense. Now, in the pros, more teams are trying to get players like him."

Few players influence their sport the way Taylor did his. Before he retired after the 1993 season, Taylor played in ten consecutive Pro Bowls—from 1981 to 1990—and led the Giants to two Super Bowl victories. Using a rare combination of quickness, strength, and primal rage, he was by far the most dominant defensive player in the 1980s. In 1994, he was named to the NFL's All-Time team.

Running back Keith Byars, who often had to try to block Taylor during the classic battles between the Eagles and Giants in the late 1980s, acknowledged Taylor's legendary status when he said, "In 30 or 40 years, I'm going to take out the tapes and show them to my kids and grandkids, to show them I really played against Lawrence Taylor, the greatest."

ABOVE: **Lawrence Taylor (56) was famous for sacking the quarterback, but he also could stop the run, as he did here against Eric Dickerson.**

OPPOSITE: **Lawrence Taylor (56) was arguably the greatest defensive player in pro football history. Teams usually tried to block him with two or three linemen.**

DERRICK THOMAS

As Lawrence Taylor's career began to wind down, Derrick Thomas took the baton from him as the NFL's premier pass-rushing linebacker. Since 1989, when he entered the NFL, no linebacker has had more sacks than Thomas. Sacks alone, however, aren't the sole measure of Thomas's capabilities. He, like all great players, has the ability to take over a game.

During his senior year at the University of Alabama, Thomas was one of the most dominant defensive players in the nation. A unanimous All-American and the Butkus Award winner as the nation's outstanding college linebacker, Thomas was selected by the Kansas City Chiefs in the first round of the 1989 NFL draft. It didn't take him long to go to work on NFL quarterbacks. In his rookie year, Thomas recorded ten sacks, made the Pro Bowl, and was named Defensive Rookie of the Year.

Lining up as the right outside linebacker, Thomas uses his tremendous speed and strength to blow by blockers on his way to the quarterback. "You watch the guy on film, he's got so much speed, tackles don't have a chance," said Miami Dolphins offensive line coach Larry Beightol. "It's almost impossible to block him."

In 1990, Thomas used that speed to lead the league with 20 sacks, the fifth-highest single-season total in NFL history. Seven of those sacks came against the Seattle Seahawks, setting an NFL single-game record. After sacking Seahawks quarterback Dave Krieg on Seattle's first two possessions, Thomas could feel that he was going to have a big game. "At that point the adrenaline was really pumping," recalled Thomas. "Then on the sidelines [Kansas City head coach Marty Schottenheimer] comes over and says, 'O.K., kid, don't

In his rookie season of 1989, Derrick Thomas (58) recorded 10 sacks in his first 10 games. Here, Thomas returns a fumble for a touchdown.

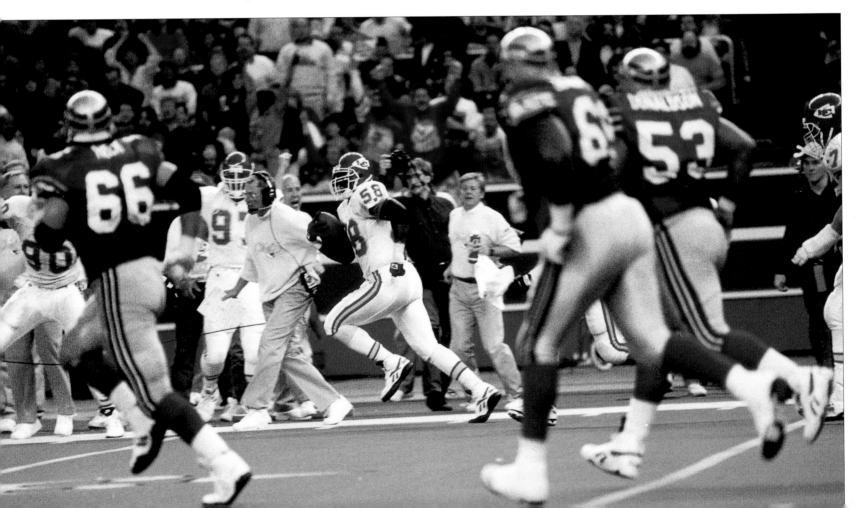

let up. Go out there and keep doing what you do best: rush.'"

Over the course of his career, Derrick Thomas has become more than simply a pass rusher. The Chiefs also rely on him to stop the run. "This is putting more pressure on him, I guess, but there's not a better linebacker in this league on the tight end," Schottenheimer said. "If people are man blocking and try to run on him, he will beat you."

To help pressure the quarterback, Thomas often lines up at defensive end in passing situations. The Chiefs coaching staff, however, made the mistake of trying to create a hybrid "rushbacker" position for Thomas in 1993. It was essentially a defensive end position, but Thomas was too small to play that position on every down. His record of eight sacks in 1993 was the lowest total of his career at that point, and the Chiefs scrapped the plan.

One criticism of Thomas is that he plays well only on artificial turf. When the Chiefs replaced Arrowhead Stadium's artificial turf with natural grass in 1994, some people expected Thomas's effectiveness to decline. Thomas quieted his critics when he sacked San Francisco 49ers quarterback Steve Young three times in a September game at Arrowhead. "And so ends the myth of the grass," Thomas said after the game. He went on to record nine of his 11 sacks that season on natural grass.

Besides sacking the quarterback and stopping the run, Thomas can also take the ball away from the offense. He has forced 32 fumbles and recovered 15 fumbles in his career. Although he has made the Pro Bowl in each of his eight NFL seasons, Thomas was inexplicably omitted from the NFL's All-Decade team of the 1990s.

Speed and quickness make Derrick Thomas an outstanding pass rusher. Thomas has made at least 10 sacks in six of his eight NFL seasons.

When Thomas' career is finally over, he will be remembered as a sack artist. It remains to be seen whether he will retire as the NFL's all-time leader in quarterback sacks. Thomas reached the 50-sack plateau in his fifty-fourth game; only Reggie White and Mark Gastineau reached that mark faster. New rules, however, that allow offensive linemen to use their hands liberally could hurt Thomas' chances of becoming the all-time sack leader. This has cut down the number of sacks in recent years across the NFL. Through the 1996 season, Thomas has 98 career sacks; White is the NFL's all-time sack leader with 165.5.

HALL OF FAME LINEBACKERS

Player	Teams	Height	Weight	Year Inducted
Chuck Bednarik[1]	Philadelphia Eagles (1949-1962)	6' 3"	235 lb.	1967
Bobby Bell[2]	Kansas City Chiefs (1963-1974)	6' 4"	230 lb.	1983
Dick Butkus	Chicago Bears (1965-1973)	6' 3"	245 lb.	1979
George Connor[3]	Chicago Bears (1948-1955)	6' 3"	240 lb.	1975
Bill George	Chicago Bears (1952-1965) Los Angeles Rams (1966)	6' 2"	230 lb.	1974
Jack Ham	Pittsburgh Steelers (1971-1982)	6' 1"	220 lb.	1988
Ted Hendricks	Baltimore Colts (1969-1973) Green Bay Packers (1974) Oakland/Los Angeles Raiders (1975-1983)	6' 7"	235 lb.	1990
Sam Huff	New York Giants (1956-1963) Washington Redskins (1964-1967, 1969)	6' 1"	230 lb.	1982
Jack Lambert	Pittsburgh Steelers (1974-1984)	6' 4"	220 lb.	1990
Willie Lanier	Kansas City Chiefs (1967-1977)	6' 1"	245 lb.	1986
Ray Nitschke	Green Bay Packers (1958-1972)	6' 3"	240 lb.	1978
Joe Schmidt	Detroit Lions (1953-1965)	6' 0"	220 lb.	1973

1-Bednarik also played center.
2-Bell also played defensive end.
3-Connor also played defensive tackle and offensive tackle.

BIBLIOGRAPHY

Allen, George, and Ben Olan. *Pro Football's 100 Greatest*, Indianapolis: Bobbs-Merrill, 1982.

Buoniconti, Nick, and Dick Anderson. *Defensive Football*. New York: Atheneum, 1974.

Capezzuto, Tom. "No Question: Norton's No. 1." *Football Digest*, May/June 1994, pp 56–60.

Christensen, Todd. "1993 Football Dream Team." *Sport*, September 1993, p. 78.

Clary, Jack. *Pro Football's Great Moments*. New York: Bonanza Books, 1983.

Curtis, Mike, and Bill Gilbert. *Keep Off My Turf*. Philadelphia: Lippincott, 1972.

Daly, Dan, and Bob O'Donnell. *The Pro Football Chronicle*. New York: Collier Books, 1990.

Dean, Rick. "All the Pieces Finally Fit for Derrick Thomas." *Football Digest*, February 1995, pp. 48–54.

Didinger, Ray. "Best of the Best." *Super Bowl XXV Program*, January 27, 1991.

Eskenazi, Gerald. "Flores Hints Team Should Stay in Oakland." *The New York Times*, January 27, 1981, pp. B15–B16.

Fleming, David. "Kevin Greene." *Sports Illustrated Presents NFL '95*, September 1995, p. 132.

Frisaro, Joe. "Will the Real Bryan Cox Please Stand Up?" *Football Digest*, February 1995, pp. 56–60.

Gigliott, Jim, and Brian Peterson. "Unlikely Heroes," *Super Bowl XXVIII Program*, January 30, 1994.

Gutman, Bill. *Gamebreakers of the NFL*. New York: Random House, 1973.

———. *New Breed Heroes of Pro Football*. New York: J. Messner, 1973.

Harrington, Denis J. *Pro Football Hall of Fame*. Jefferson, NC: McFarland, 1991.

Hickok, Ralph. *The Pro Football Fan's Companion*. New York: Macmillan, 1995.

Huff, Sam, and Leonard Shapiro. *Tough Stuff*. New York: St. Martin's Press, 1988.

Johnson, Paul M. "Super Bowl Dream Team." *Sport*, February 1996, pp. 22–24.

Judge, Clark. "Defensive Player of the Year: Junior Seau." *Football Digest*, April 1993, pp. 30–34.

King, Peter. "Da Hibernating Bears." *Sports Illustrated*, November 30, 1992, p. 66.

———. "He'll Be Missed." *Sports Illustrated*, November 16, 1992, p. 61.

———. "Jim Brown." *Sports Illustrated*, September 19, 1994, p. 56.

———, "Still in the Hunt." *Sports Illustrated*, November 27, 1995, p. 40.

Kirkpatrick, Curry. "Duck, Blitzburgh's Back." *Newsweek*, January 9, 1995, p. 63.

Korch, Rick. *The Truly Great*. Dallas: Taylor Publishing Company, 1993.

LaBlanc, Michael, ed. *Professional Sports Teams Histories: Football*. Detroit: Gale Research, 1994.

Labriola, Bob. "Kevin Greene: He's All That He Can Be." *Football Digest*, November 1993, pp. 62–66.

Lamb, Kevin, and C. Mortensen. "The NFL's Best." *Sport*, October 1991, pp. 51–52.

Lieber, Jill. "Hard Charger." *Sports Illustrated*, September 6, 1993, p. 64.

———. "Invincible? No, Just Real Mean." *Sports Illustrated*, January 26, 1987, pp. 36–41.

———. "Kiss That Past Goodbye." *Sports Illustrated*, September 6, 1993, p. 104.

Litsky, Frank. "Cowboys' Defense Pours On Pressure." *The New York Times*, February 1, 1993.

Lyon, Bill. "Taylor Is Lethal, And Loves It." *Philadelphia Inquirer*, January 25, 1987, p. C1.

Madden, John, and Dave Anderson. *Hey Wait a Minute (I Wrote a Book!)*. New York: Villard Books, 1984.

———. *One Knee Equals Two Feet*. New York: Villard Books, 1986.

McDermott, John R. "The Year of the Rookie." *Life*, November 5, 1965, pp. 72–80.

Michael, Paul. *Professional Football's Greatest Games*. Englewood Cliffs, NJ: Prentice-Hall, 1972.

Miller, J. David. *The Super Book of Football*. Boston: Little, Brown, 1990.

Mullin, John. "The Up-and-Comers." *The Sporting News*, October 9, 1995, pp. 11–12.

Murphy, Austin. "Paup Fiction." *Sports Illustrated*, March 4, 1996.

———. "Spittin' Venom." *Sports Illustrated*, January 29, 1996, pp. 174–178.

Neff, Craig. "The Brawny and Brainy Bears." *Sports Illustrated*, November 26, 1984, pp. 116–119.

Neft, David S., and Richard M. Cohen. *The Pro Football Encyclopedia*. New York: St. Martin's Press, 1990.

O'Shei, Tim. "It's Time To Give Bryce Paup A Little Respect." *Football Digest*, March 1996, pp. 72–76.

Parcells, Bill, and Mike Lupica. *Parcells*. Chicago: Bonus Books, 1987.

Peterson, Mark. "Derrick Thomas: Sack Man." *Boys Life*, October 1992, pp. 12–15.

Platt, Larry. "From the Old School." *Sport*, July 1992, pp. 29–31.

Pompei, Dan. "The Butkus-Nitschke Rivalry Still Is a Big Hit." *Football Digest*, March 1995, pp. 68–72.

Porter, David L, ed. *Biographical Dictionary of American Sports: Football*. New York: Greenwood Press, 1987.

Reid, Ron. "On the NFL." *Philadelphia Inquirer*, May 19, 1996, p. 2.

Reilly, Rick. "These Bills Stack Up." *Sports Illustrated*, December 7, 1987, pp. 66–70.

Schulian, John. "Concrete Charlie." *Sports Illustrated*, September 6, 1993, p. 74.

Silver, Michael. "The Waning of a Legend." *Sports Illustrated*, December 11, 1995, p. 24.

Singletary, Mike, and Armen Keteyian. *Calling the Shots*. Chicago: Contemporary Books, 1986.

Stellino, Vito. "Quarterbacks Beware: These Guys Can Hurt You," *Football Digest*, January 1996, pp. 66–71.

———. "Same Game, Different Scheme." *Football Digest*, December 1995, pp. 30–34.

Stroud, Rick. "All Nickerson Wants Is a Little Respect." *Football Digest*, November 1994, pp. 65–70.

Sullivan, George. *All About Football*. New York: Dodd, Mead, 1987.

———. *Pro Football's All-Time Greats*. New York: G.P. Putnam's Sons, 1968.

Tarkenton, Elaine, and Michael Rich. *A Wife's Guide To Pro Football*. New York: Viking, 1969.

Tatum, Kevin, and Tim Panaccio. "On the NFL." *Philadelphia Inquirer*, June 16, 1995.

Taylor, Lawrence, and David Falkner. *LT: Living on the Edge*. New York: Times Books, 1987.

Telander, Rick. "The Last Angry Men." *Sports Illustrated*, September 6, 1993, p. 54.

———. "Linebacker Music." *Sports Illustrated*, September 9, 1987.

———. "Pittsburgh's Bashful Bruiser." *Sports Illustrated*, November 19, 1984, pp. 78–80.

Thomas, Jim. "The Book On...Roman Phifer." *The Sporting News*, September 18, 1995.

Weinberg, Rick. "Hotshot: Kevin Greene." *Sport*, September 1995, p. 52.

Weisman, Larry. "No Ironman He, Scoffs Bednarik." *USA Today*, September 6, 1996, p. 3.

Wiley, Ralph. "Like Father, Like Son." *Sports Illustrated*, October 12, 1987, pp. 74–80.

Wilner, Barry. "The '95 Season Belonged to the Men Who Catch the Ball." *Football Digest*, April 1996, pp. 34–44.

———. "Just Be Glad You Don't Have To Play These Guys." *Football Digest*, November 1995, pp. 16–24.

Zimmerman, Paul. "The Best Athletes on the Field." *Sports Illustrated*, September 4, 1985, pp. 136–149.

———. "Big D, As In Dynasty." *Sports Illustrated*, February 8, 1993.

———. "Charged-Up Defense." *Sports Illustrated*, December 21, 1992, p. 28.

———. "Getting Set To Soar." *Sports Illustrated*, September 3, 1986, pp. 127–138.

———. "Hendricks," *Sports Illustrated*, October 17, 1983, pp. 94–106.

———. "Like Old Times." *Sports Illustrated*, November 15, 1993, p. 28.

———. "LT on LT." *Sports Illustrated*, September 16, 1991, pp. 40–48.

———. "No Names No More." *Sports Illustrated*, November 16, 1992.

———. "A Rose By Any Other Name." *Sports Illustrated*, July 30, 1984, pp. 26–40.

———. "Shoot-Out in Kansas City." *Sports Illustrated*, September 19, 1994, p. 24.

———. "Super Bowl XVIII." *Sports Illustrated*, January 30, 1984, pp. 14–29.

———. "What If...." *Sports Illustrated*, January 30, 1995, p. 54.

PHOTOGRAPHY CREDITS

INDEX